*The crescent moon amid her sisters bright
turns forth a silver lining on the night;
and wheels Time's circling shadow round
on leaf-tide bud and winter-hardened ground.
Visions are of a moment made,
dream of a dream, shadow of a shade.*

SUSAN POWER

the dreamcatcher

an A-Z guide to your dreams and what they mean

Philip Clucas MSIAD

THUNDER BAY
P·R·E·S·S

Published in the United States by
Thunder Bay Press
An imprint of the Advantage Publishers Group
5880 Oberlin Drive, San Diego, CA 92121-4794
www.advantagebooksonline.com

All notations of errors or omissions should be
addressed to Thunder Bay Press, editorial
department, at the above address. All other
correspondence (author inquiries, permissions)
concerning the content of this book should be
addressed to Salamander Books Limited, 8
Blenheim Court, Brewery Road, London N7
9NY, England.

ISBN 1-57145-569-8
Library of Congress Cataloging-in-Publication
Data available upon request.
  2 3 4 5 01 02 03 04

The information in this book is true and
complete to the best of our knowledge. All
recommendations are made without any
guarantee on the part of the author or
publisher, who also disclaim any liability incurred
in connection with the use of this data or
specific details.

Philip Clucas is an artist, writer, and designer who has worked in publishing and design for more than 25 years. He is the author of several books including *Country Seasons, Above Britain, England's Churches, Wonders of the World* and *Britain: This Beautiful Land*.

He has also written many poetry books, including a series of 24 inspirational titles (under the pseudonym 'Susan Power') which achieved combined sales in excess of 2.5 million copies, one of the largest print runs ever recorded for a living poet.

He has long been fascinated by the symbolism of dreams and the world of the imagination, He has made a special study of, and lectured on, the mystical poet and artist William Blake and his 'disciple', the Victorian visionary painter Samuel Palmer. He lives in Kent, England with his wife and three children.

CREDITS

WRITTEN AND DESIGNED: **Philip Clucas** MSIAD

EDITOR: **Philip de Ste. Croix**

PUBLISHING EDITOR: **Will Steeds**

RESEARCH ASSISTANT: **Douglas Clucas**

PHOTOGRAPHS: **Digital Vision**

ADDITIONAL PHOTOGRAPHY AND ILLUSTRATION: **Jack Clucas**
(pages 17, 18, 123, 186, 244-245, 289 and 343)

PRODUCED BY TOPPAN

PRINTED IN CHINA

The Bridgeman Art Library *(page 127 – courtesy of The Victoria and Albert Museum, London; page 253 – Private Collection; page 336 – courtesy of The Fitzwilliam Museum, Cambridge)*

Contents

· ·

Introduction

Dreams have been a source of wonderment to humankind throughout the centuries – a fact that is hardly surprising given that each and every one of us spends, on average, a third of our lives in that mysterious realm of our own imagining, where waking consciousness can but dimly penetrate.

Our need for sleep as a revitalizing element for body and mind is beyond question. Most of us experience a distinctive sleeping pattern that follows a set cycle – a rhythm of sleep that progresses through about 90-minute cycles, which can be divided into four recordable segments when monitored by an electroencephalograph (ECG) machine. The first quarter-phase is the lightest sleep we experience. Our muscles relax, breathing becomes shallow and our heart beat slows down. Next, we enter a realm of deeper sleep in which sleep-walking and sleep-talking *(somniloquence)* are most likely to manifest themselves. In the third quarter of the cycle our body temperature falls by several degrees, and in this mode it becomes extremely difficult to awaken the sleeper. The fourth and final stage is the deepest level of sleep, and one that is likely to last for about 30 minutes. Once this "deepest mode" has run its course we swing back to the first phase again. It is usually at this moment of re-entry to the lightest stage of sleep that dreaming begins.

Our mind employs the symbolic representations of smell, sound, touch, taste, and sight in dreaming, but by far the most striking and vivid are the visual images it presents – accompanied by noticeable "rapid eye movement." The dreams engendered are now generally accepted to serve a variety of purposes in our lives. They mirror the sleeper's recent waking experiences, whether trivial or traumatic, but combine them in the dreamscape with images that can dredge the long-distant past for unresolved conflicts and emotions. This combination can present us with a worrying or surreal world which is infinitely varied and frequently strange. Such dreams serve to alert us to problems, release inner tensions and – when harnessed by the receptive imagination – can inspire the spirit to artistic or literary achievement.

The unconscious mind has an uncanny knack of pinpointing topics that our conscious mind has either overlooked or refuses (through self-censorship) to acknowledge. It frequently implants these symbols into our dreams to enable us to confront and resolve specific problems. By its nature each dream is unique to the individual but – because we all share similar experiences within our cultures – there are certain standard dream symbols that are common to all. The meanings of these symbols are analyzed within the pages of *The Dreamcatcher* (pages 38-395). It is hoped that their interpretation will shed a little more light upon the dreamer's innermost feelings and thus enable him or her to reach a greater understanding, and appreciation of, their "inner-psyche."

Dream Beliefs

The interpretation of dreams has been practiced by humankind since time immemorial. Dreams are seen to possess an awesome significance that all civilizations have sought to understand or analyze in the light of their pervading beliefs and customs.

To the Ancient World dreams were seen as a "bridge" between mundane existence and the realms of the gods. Dreams were generally considered to fall into three categories – those in which the gods demanded pious obedience, dreams of prophetic warning, and those of divine revelation. A common supposition was that dreams needed to be "incubated" (from the latin *incubare* meaning *"to lie down upon"*) and people would visit sanctuaries or shrines to sleep before the deity on a "dream bed" in the hope of receiving divine healing or advice through the medium of their dreams.

The Hebrews, being monotheistic, considered dreams to be the voice of one God alone. The Old Testament is peppered with dream revelations. The Biblical prophets also incubated their dreams – notable examples being Samuel who *"lay down and slept in the temple of Shiloh before the Ark and received the world of the Lord,"* and Solomon who went to a high place where *"the Lord appeared in a dream by night"* and God said *"Ask what I shall give thee."* Perhaps the most famous dreamer, however, appears in the Book of Genesis, where Pharaoh's vision of seven fat, and seven lean, cows is interpreted by Joseph to portend future events in the Land of Egypt.

Religion and dreamlore seem happily to co-exist in many cultures. In Mohammed's sacred book distinction is made between "true dreams" coming from God, and false dreams. Hindus set great store by "sleeping wisdom;" and Australian Aborigines have, at the heart of their mythology, a creation story that centers upon the "Dreamtime" – when sleeping spirits arose and wandered the Earth shaping the landscape and singing the names of everything into being, before subsiding once again into an underworld of sleep.

Many Native American tribes believe that dreams bring to light the concealed and unknown wishes of the soul. It was always the most vivid dreamer who was chosen as the shaman, and through his dreams and sleep-like trances he was able to understand the many and varied languages of mammal, reptile, and bird – indeed..."*could hear the very earth singing.*"

Making a DreamCatcher

To Native Americans, the circle symbolizes the cyclical nature of traditional cosmology. They believe that the Earth is a circle, below which is the circle of the sky, and inside these circles there are powerful spiritual centers. For this reason a dreamcatcher is circular, with a powerful center.

If hung over the bed it reputedly prevents evil from entering the soul of a sleeping person. As bad thoughts try to intrude into the mind, the spiritual circle catch them as if in a net, and so protects the sleeper from nightmares and helps to promote peaceful rest.

Decorating a dreamcatcher with favorite feathers, stones, shells, and other objects gathered from nature further empowers it to protect its owner, or the person for whom the dreamcatcher is created.

YOU WILL NEED

- thick wire
- masking tape
- 6ft (1.8m) of bias binding
- all-purpose household glue
- thick thread
- 4ft (1.2m) of suede thonging
- 30 large-holed wooden beads
- a selection of feathers

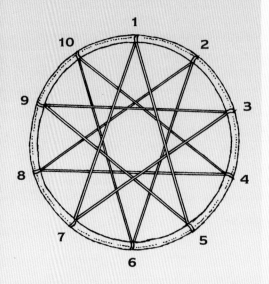

1 Bend the thick wire into a circle about 8 inches (20cm) in diameter. Overlap the wire's ends and join them together with masking tape. Bind the whole length of the circle with bias binding and glue the end of the tape onto the ring.

2 Divide the ring into tenths and mark each position with a pen. To make the web, tie the thread to the ring at position 1. Take the thread to position 5 and tie it into place. Continue winding on the thread to positions 9, 3 and 7 before returning it to position 1 and tie into place. You should now have a five-pointed star within the ring.

3 Make another five-pointed star using positions 2, 6, 10, 4 and 8 before securing the thread at position 2 again. During this process a few beads or other found objects can be attached to the thread and woven into the star's framework.

4 Tie a length of suede thong to the top of the circle at position 1 and decorate the hanging ends with beads glued into place on the suede thong.

5 Lengths of thong can now be strung from positions 4, 5, 6, 7 and 8. Decorate these thongs with beads then finish off each suede thong with a feather. The feather can be glued to the thong and held in place with a bead.

Note: smaller or larger dreamcatchers can be created by altering the diameter of the ring.

Lucid Dreams and Inspiration

One of the most interesting aspects of dreamlore is the discovery that you can harness dreams to stimulate your own creative forces. This is facilitated by "lucid dreaming" – a process whereby the sleeper suddenly realizes that they are in fact dreaming; when this occurs every aspect of the dream takes on a new dimension. The mind shows the same consciousness as when it is awake, and by learning to control events in lucid dreaming you can indulge in wish-fulfilment, and experience problem-solving dreams that can instil a sense of satisfaction and achievement that linger long after the dreamer has woken.

The exciting prospect that sleepers can exert a degree of control over their own dreams and can influence their outcome means that nightmares may often be turned back against themselves. Thus, by realizing that you are having a troubled dream, you can often deflect its malign force against itself. This allows you to work through a nightmare – by facing up to your own personal demons you should be able to resolve the conflict within yourself that produces the terrifying images. Hostile phantoms in dreams represent sides of our psyche that we choose to deny – by confronting them fully in lucid dreaming they can be neutralized and integrated.

Artists, musicians, writers, inventors, and scientists have all acknowledged the role that lucid dreaming plays as a source of creative inspiration. William Shakespeare's works are littered with allusions to the dreamscape; while Samuel Taylor Coleridge's poem *Kubla Khan* was conceived during an opium-induced sleep. On waking the poet hurried to his desk to write it down, but was called upon to answer a knock at the door. On returning, all that remained of his "vision" were tantalizing fragments and dim reflections "*...all the rest was lost like images on the surface of a stream.*" This incident serves

Charles Dickens derived inspiration for many of his characters from the realms of dreams. One day he visited Cooling churchyard near his home in Rochester, Kent, where he noted in passing the graves of 13 children from one family. That night in a dream he ascribed the sad tombs to the brothers and sisters of Pip, and thus was forged the kernel of the plot of Great Expectations.

to demonstrate the importance of recording a dream, not only immediately upon waking but without interruption too.

The Italian composer Giuseppe Tartini entitled one of his pieces *The Devil's Sonata* after he remembered a musical *trill* from a dream in which the devil played the violin to him. Mozart was adamant that he composed his finest works while dreaming; and ex-Beatle Paul McCartney awoke one morning, went straight to his piano and played the complete tune (not just a few bars) of one of the biggest selling records of all time – *Yesterday*.

The haunting metamorphosis of Dr. Jekyll into Mr. Hyde was inspired within the dreamscape of Robert Louis Stevenson's sleeping mind; while the profoundly psychic and psychological "adventures" that befell Alice sprang from the lucid dreaming of her creator Charles Lutwidge Dodgson, better known as Lewis Carroll.

The English novelist Graham Greene was yet another in a long line of dream-inspired authors. In the 1980s he told an audience at a prize-giving ceremony that his books *"write themselves in the dead of night."* He apparently woke several times to record outlines of dreams that later formed the basis of his novels. *"If I'm really working I re-read what I've written during the day before I go to bed and the problems are solved in my sleep."* He went on to reveal that he kept a diary of his dreams in which he meticulous recorded insights and story lines offered up by his unshackled mind.

Sweet Dreams

D reams require sleep, and sleep demands that both body and mind be properly relaxed. Here are my ten suggestions for achieving a good night's sleep and the prospect of creating "sweet dreams."

1 Try not to worry that you get too little sleep – this is very rarely the case. Most people not only overestimate their need for sleep, but they also underestimate the amount of sleep they actually get during a "sleepless night."

2 Ensure that you take some form of physical exercise during the day

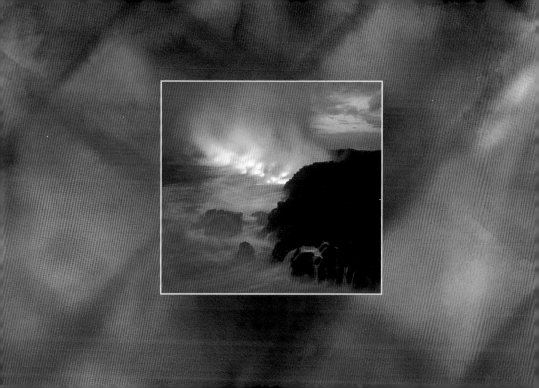

so that your body craves rest at night. Even a short stroll in the fresh air before you go to bed is better than no exercise at all.

3 Set the mood for sleep by relaxing in a warm bath half an hour before you retire to bed. Do not be tempted to take a brisk shower as this might prove too invigorating.

4 Try to allow three hours between your last meal and the onset of sleep. Nightmares are sometimes blamed on troubled digestion, and your dreams may reflect this problem with strange and alarming visions.

5 Avoid stimulating a body that is preparing to rest. Caffeine, nicotine, and alcohol all suppress the rapid eye movement associated with dreaming. These drugs also inhibit the deeper stages of sleep.

6 Ensure that your bed is comfortable and that the room is sufficiently dark – light is the natural cue for waking. Eliminate as much background noise as possible. You can muffle noise you have no control over by gentle tape recordings of waterfalls or surf breaking on a tropical beach.

7 Make sure that you are neither too hot nor too cold. A room temperature of 60°-65°F (16°-18°C) is considered comfortable for sleep. The room should be well aired to avoid it getting stuffy.

8 Never take your work to bed with you. If worrying thoughts enter your head and refuse to leave, jot them down on a bedside notepad, then consider the matter closed until you re-visit them in the morning.

9 Read yourself to sleep. Fond memories of a parent reading to us at bedtime can be recaptured by escaping once again into the world of the written word. This will distance you from the anxieties of the past day. If the book proves too absorbing, however, swop it for one that is guaranteed to calm the mind.

10 If you wake during the night to pervasive thoughts that crowd out sleep, you are unlikely to banish them by simply "thinking of nothing" – the mind, like nature, abhors a vacuum. Instead try a simple relaxation exercise. Make yourself comfortable in bed, tense the toes on your left foot and hold the tension for five seconds, then release and tell youself how relaxed your toes now feel. In this manner proceed from left to right-hand side, taking it in turns to work your way up the muscle groups of your legs, buttocks, hips, back, hands, arms, and finally, the head. In each instant try to appreciate the release of tension. The distraction of the exercise and the relaxation it creates should be sufficiently distracting to let you drift off to sleep.

Finally, if all else fails, get out of bed and make yourself a warm milky drink. This is preferable to simply lying there restlessly tossing and turning. In fact, you might break the cycle of persistent insomnia by making a point, on one occasion, of staying up and refusing to return to bed.

Recording Your Dreams

We all experience many and varied dreams during the course of a night's sleep, but the vast majority are destined to fade and vanish the instant we wake. If you keep a pencil and notepaper beside your bed, however, and manage to jot down a few of the events that occurred in your dream, you will be able, with practice, to remember more and more about its content and the events depicted.

Resist the distractions of the coming day and try to set aside a few moments to recall and note down what you remember about the dream. Later you can transfer the information to an 'official' dream

A dream diary is a useful tool in interpreting the significance and meaning of your subconscious thoughts. By tabulating your dreams in a methodical manner, related themes and patterns emerge over the course of weeks and months.

DREAM DIARY

Date of dream: _____

Day of the week:: _____

People involved in the dream: _____

_____

Mood and feelings expressed: _____

_____

Prominent colors: _____

_____

What story did the dream enact?: _____

_____

_____

Problems and conflicts encountered: _____

_____

How were problems dealt with?: _____

_____

Did the dream occur in the past or present?: _____

_____

Prominent symbols: _____

_____

Repeated elements from past dreams: _____

_____

How did the dream end?: _____

_____

Conclusions: _____

_____

diary using your original jottings as an *aide memoire*. By recording your dreams in this manner in line with set criteria (as shown in the example on the opposite page) you will be prompted to explore the dream in greater detail. It is surprising just how much of the dream's original content can be remembered using this method.

When you look back over the diary's entries you will discover significant patterns emerging. The permanent record that you have created will give you a significant insight into your deepest desires and emotions, through which you can experience greater self-knowledge.

After a while you will learn to tailor the diary format to reflect the 'prompts' that serve you best. Those shown left are simply suggestions.

The Symbolism of Dreams

"Two dreams are never the same, nor are two flowers ever alike"

On the following pages *The DreamCatcher* presents a collection of more than 340 of the most commonly encountered symbols that constitute the language of dreams accompanied by explanatory text that provides the latest, most widely accepted interpretations of what these images mean.

Consult the following alphabetical list of symbols whenever you are intrigued by the particular subject matter of a dream, but remember that dreams are, by their very nature, unique to the individual. A general interpretation of a symbol's meaning will be influenced by the overall context of that dream, and the dreamer's personal situation. Thus, no guide to dream symbolism can ever offer complete insights or definitive answers. Rather, *The DreamCatcher* should be used to help you tease out understanding of the likely significance of the various dream elements encountered by your sleeping mind.

Dreams can be regarded as "windows on the subconscious mind," and through them we can view our innermost feelings and creative thoughts in a way that allows us to confront and, hopefully, resolve problems in our waking lives.

Accident

Dreams of accidents can be very disturbing, and while the events foreseen may be a premonition of a real accident (against which you should take reasonable precautions for the next few days), it is far more likely that your subconscious mind is worrying about some aspect of your life that it fears may be about to come crashing down around you. It views your current state with concern, and thus calls up graphic images designed to shock you into appropriate action.

An alternative explanation for dreams involving accidents claims that they are your mind's way of punishing you for what it perceives to be slack or woolly thinking.

Admiration

We all like to feel admired, and a dream that you are the object of admiration is a common one. Of course, it could simply indicate vanity, but it is more likely to be a sign of confidence, denoting that you will retain the esteem of others even though you move on. If you admire someone else in your dream – possibly a person whom you dislike – it cautions that he or she may well have qualities that you have hitherto overlooked.

Adultery

Adultery and giving way to temptation is one of the oldest topics in dream lore. Despite its wider implications of being caught and emotionally compromised, the dream is usually only concerned with the fear of being confronted with some petty misdemeanor you may once have committed. Not surprisingly, to resist committing adultery is an omen of temporary disappointment.

Aircraft

In a dreamscape an aircraft is considered to be a sign of swift success. However, its power to leave the Earth's surface, and the consequent threat of falling, should caution the dreamer to beware of taking undue risk. To be a passenger in an aircraft may presage the receiving of good news, but if it crashes this suggests – not an imminent accident – but a major failure in your business dealings.

Alien (abduction)

Unlikely as it might seem, a dream about extraterrestrial abduction is usually a wish-fulfilment dream in which concerns regarding personal safety are banished once the alien is seen to be benign and of superior intelligence. The abductee may respond like a small child who idolizes a parent, and an element of conceit can sometimes enter the equation as the dreamer rejoices in the fact that it is "they" whom the being has chosen.

Altar

Traditionally an altar is a symbol of purity, and to see one in a dream implies the discovery of inner peace in your life, both now and in the future. To stand with your back to an altar, however, forebodes approaching sorrows.

Anchor

To see an anchor in a dream is an encouragement to develop a stronger attachment to a person or place, and so reintroduce stability to your life. Alternatively, it may suggest that a lover whose affections you have recently doubted really does care for you, and circumstances will soon make this welcome fact apparent.

Angel

Predictably, the appearance of these celestial winged entities in a dream is an extremely propitious sign that denotes wisdom and protection. They may be seen as dream messengers, or "guardian angels," and their advice, if given to you in a dream, should be acted upon. To a religious person, a vision of an angel will serve to reinforce and strengthen existing beliefs; others may take encouragement and consolation from the fact they have a spiritual guardian who has their best wishes at heart and will watch over them.

The emotion of anger implies that your freedom has been stifled in waking life, and resentment still breeds in your dreams. It can foretell a quarrel, or an attack upon your character. If someone is angry with the dreamer, and you deflect this with composure, it portends that you will conciliate between opposing factions, earning the gratitude of both.

Anger

Anxiety

Anxiety dreams invariably relate to waking worries and stress. Whatever causes such problems in life can be reduced if you try to make the best of circumstances. Remember that no-one has everything, and everyone has some element of sorrow intermingled with the happiness of life – the trick is to make the laughter outweigh the tears.

Apes and Monkeys

Rather unfairly, these creatures have come to be regarded as symbols of deceit and meddling behavior. To dream of an ape implies regressive tendencies and is, perhaps, an implied criticism of the dreamer's own previous bad or lewd behavior. Monkeys, on the other hand, serve to warn the sleeper that he or she is surrounded by liars and false friends. A woman who dreams of feeding a monkey may be seduced by flattery.

Apple

Apples have a strong sexual connotation – stemming from the serpent's original temptation of Eve with this fruit in the Garden of Eden. Thus to dream of eating an apple is generally regarded as showing a desire to fulfil sexual appetite – literally to taste the full fruits of life. However, just as Eve was deceived by the serpent, so dreamers should be wary of the consequences of their amorous activities, for by grasping the proffered fruit with open hands, you may let what you already hold slip through your fingers. Apples also caution the dreamer that today's actions will bring future consequences.

Arrow

Despite being a weapon of war, the arrow is a surprisingly positive symbol – of sunlight, and of the love-smitten ... the target is within sight so the dreamer should take aim and go for it! Depending on the context, the arrow may express a wish to have a sexual relationship with a person you admire. Conversely it could express a desire to injure them. To aim and miss the target may indicate that you will experience difficulties in your relationships, where love falls "wide of the mark."

Asparagus

Perceived as an aphrodisiac, to dream of eating asparagus with its phallic overtones is seen as a desire for lust – an idea echoed in "The Perfumed Garden" which notes that it *"causes the virile member to be on the alert, night and day."*

Automobile

Were you the driver or the passenger? ... An automobile is a dream symbol with many convoluted interpretations depending upon circumstance. To be driven could indicate a need to have one's problems taken over and sorted out by another person, often a parental figure. Alternatively, to take a positive hold of the wheel and drive oneself signifies a desire to exercise control over your own destiny.

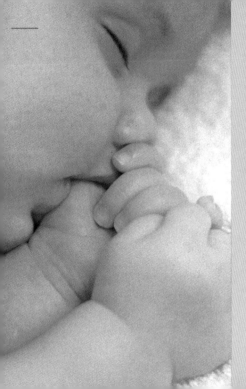

Baby

To dream of a baby may reflect a desire to look after and nurture an actual infant, but it more usually stands as a symbol of "self" – a yearning by the dreamer for simplicity, and a return to a less-complicated time when they were guaranteed protection from helplessness. They may feel exhausted by repeated failure, and the dream is a way of escaping from the treadmill of life by stepping back to a time of supreme contentment, when everything was done for you. Regressive dreams such as sucking milk are among the happiest and most carefree that we can enjoy.

Back

A foreign land to most, our own backs are areas where our eyes cannot travel, save with the aid of film or reflection. It is little wonder, therefore, that in our dreamscapes the back is regarded as an omen of caution – a warning to take guard against threats of deceit and double-dealing. To dream of seeing a naked back denotes feelings of helplessness; whereas to see a person turn their back on you indicates that their envy may cause you harm.

The skirl of pipe # Bagpipes
music may be
evoked by distant echoes from
your ancestry – forgotten celtic
roots perhaps! It is a dream that
builds bridges between you and
the long-vanished past.

Banana
If you dream you
are eating a
banana, it is a sign of growing
prosperity. Beware the discarded
skin, however – for that which
brings wealth can also bring the
uncertainties of misfortune.

In the symbolism of **Bathing** dreams bathing has been associated with purification since early times. The image does not represent a desire for physical cleanliness so much as an act of atonement – a desire to "wash away" past indiscretions. To bathe in clear water is a good omen, but if the water is dirty, it foretells shame and sorrow. If you are in trouble and dream of bathing in the sea, it is a sure sign that your misfortune will shortly be over, and that fate will smile upon you in the near-future.

Battle

The consensus of opinion regarding a dream featuring a battle suggests that it is a warning about deep-seated grievances that need to be aired. To be on the victorious side bodes well for the dreamer, but to be defeated in battle indicates that others will ride roughshod over your plans. The dream may also serve to warn of threatening times ahead.

To dream of the carnage of battle (left) can be a powerful omen either for good or ill – depending upon your personal courage and conduct, or the severity of the injury you sustain.

For a woman to **Beauty**
dream that she
is beautiful, or a man to
imagine himself excessively
handsome, is a subconscious
warning to us to beware the
conceit of pride; it cautions
against self-delusion. That
which appears to flatter the
dreamer carries a message to the
contrary – it reveals fear of losing one's
looks due to infirmity or advancing age.
To dream of the beauty of another
person is a happier portent, and implies
a secret admirer who may soon reveal
their passionate feelings.

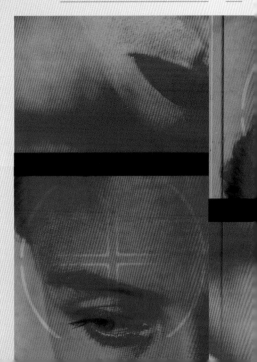

The bee is seen as industrious and hardworking, and carries the hidden promise of sweetness. The appearance of bees in a dream offers the prospect of extreme good fortune, especially if they fly around a hive in an orchard. However, should a bee sting you, the omens are reversed!

Bees

Bells

To hear the joyous sound of bells presages impending good news. However, if a solitary bell sounds a somber note, this warns the dreamer of difficulties ahead, but with the consolation that someone of a spiritual nature is looking over you.

Bicycle

Dreams involving riding a bicycle usually focus upon expending physical effort and the dreamer's final destination. They can be viewed as a metaphor for how the "rider" regards his journey through life – either as an uphill effort (signifying bright prospects through hard work), or downhill free-wheeling (easy options but with dangers ahead). Other obvious images involve cycle races, or dreaming of having no brakes.

Bird

We envy birds their powers of flight, and in dreams they have become symbols of personal freedom. A vision of a flock of birds is a sign of prosperity, and those with beautiful plumage presage favorable news. However, to kill or harm a bird indicates sorrow caused by an erring partner.

Caged birds have metaphorically had their wings clipped and, robbed of the powerful symbolism of flight, they appear in dreams as omens of drudgery. They denote an imagination hemmed in, or constrained by circumstance.

Blood is symbolic of the life-force, and in some religions it is held to

Blood

be sacred. To see yourself bleeding in a dream is usually considered a bad omen, suggesting that someone, or something, is depleting the dreamer's spiritual force. Spilt blood could indicated inner sacrifice – where the burden of worrying abut a relative or friend has "drained the person dry" of their psychic energy. Images of bleeding may be taken to indicate that you fear the loss of your own strength, and the possible enmity of a colleague who will exploit your weakness. An adolescent girl dreaming of shedding blood represents menstruation and her growth into womanhood.

Blossom

Following hard on Winter's retreat, the frothy pink or white flowerheads of trees in blossom are a welcome herald of the advancing Spring. To dream of boughs laden with the weight of their own blossom is an enchanting omen of happiness and contentment, but not necessarily of permanence.

Boat

Boats signify a journey, and in dream lore they are generally understood to represent our passage through life, or destiny. The circumstances in which the vessel is seen usually govern the omens. Smooth or "plain sailing" bodes well; but stormy seas indicate unhappy changes in life. If you are a lone traveler it could indicate a difficulty in relating to others, while "missing the boat" literally indicates a failure to grasp the deeper implications of events.

Book

If you imagine reading a book in a dream, try to remember its name, or the gist of its contents, as this will aid interpretation when you wake. The book may symbolize a thirst for knowledge, and should always be taken as a positive omen for anyone with creative or literary aspirations. However, a half-empty bookshelf indicates that the dreamer's hopes outweigh his or her talent.

Boss

To see your boss (or similar authoritarian figure) in a dream implies you are feeling vulnerable and mentally uncertain. If the boss is pleasant, it shows you are being over-sensitive; but to incur displeasure or criticism portends stormy times in which you must remain calm under pressure, and never rise to their bait.

Bread

Bread, "the staff of life," is treated with reverence in many cultures, and it is considered a breach of natural law to harm any person with whom you have sat down and broken bread. In dream lore, bread also expresses many of the ancient qualities with which it was honored, and is now seen as a talisman of peace and health if encountered in the realms of sleep. By association, baking and bakers are also regarded as being favorable omens, and it is likely that a problem will resolve itself if you dream of either. A rise in status, or salary, may also be indicated.

Bridge

The dream symbolism of the bridge represents the passage from one stage of your life to the next; it may indicate a mental transition just as much as a physical one. The bridge's construction and state of repair will indicate the degree of danger, or difficulty, the dreamer faces on the journey.

Butcher / Meat

The omens relating to these closely associated topics are far from propitious. Butchers symbolize latent anger and pent-up aggression; while meat highlights the "sins of the flesh" – of dead carcasses devoid of the living soul.

" We are the music makers,
We are the dreamers of dreams "

"We are the music makers,
*   We are the dreamers of dreams,*
Wandering by lone sea-breakers,
*   And sitting by desolate streams.*
World-losers and world-forsakers,
*   On whom the pale moon gleams:*
We are the movers and shakers
*   Of the world for ever, it seems...*

...For each age is a dream that is dying,
*   Or one that is coming to birth."*

ARTHUR O'SHAUGHNESSY 1844–81

Butterfly

The butterfly is invariably perceived as a positive symbol for the dreamer, and represents the magical powers of transformation and renewal – as exemplified by its emergence from the death-like confines of its cocoon to the fragile, perishable beauty of its life

on the wing. To see a butterfly in a dream could indicate an inability to settle down and accept responsibilities on the part of the sleeper, or perhaps a deeper yearning to be free of mundane restrictions. Spiritually, a butterfly dream signifies the psyche's desire to move forward to greater spiritual awareness.

Cabbage

In the vast pantheon of dream symbolism it might be thought that the cabbage occupies a place of peripheral importance, but this is far from true. It is esteemed a highly favorable dream portent if cabbages are seen being planted (representing the acquisition of wisdom) or tended in the field (a sign of inner strengths). If, however, you dream of the heads of cabbages being cut for harvest, it denotes that you will tighten the noose of calamity around your own neck by reckless spending.

Cage

A dream of being put in a cage symbolizes areas of the dreamer's life in which they feel trapped. The sleeper may be unable to rid themselves of inhibitions, and would benefit from a more relaxed approach to life, enabling them to examine their feelings with greater freedom. Alternatively, the dreamer may feel restricted by the constraints of friends or family ties.

Dreams featuring caged song birds traditionally symbolize the death of innocence, and to dream of an empty cage with an open door – lost virginity.

Calm

If calm and serenity pervade your dreamscape, this should naturally be regarded as a sign of great good fortune; it denotes that a period of travail has passed over, and a new era of tranquility is about to begin. To dream that you remain calm in the face of imminent danger represents ideas or personal projects that have become unsustainable.

By imagining a calm scene similar to that shown opposite, the dreamer can, with practice, alter the atmosphere of a disconcerting dream, giving it a softer, more pleasant and tranquil aspect.

However pleasant the dream may seem, to be given candy

Candy

in recognition of achievement means that you are indulging in appreciation of your own abilities in a rather conceited way.

Cannon

Overpoweringly masculine in symbolism, a cannon is believed to be an omen of future problems – perhaps brought about by too many worries that remain unaddressed. In dreams, a

common theme is an inability to load and fire the cannon at advancing enemies. This image emphasizes the extent of one's problems, and the fact that they must be dealt with as soon as possible.

To dream of playing **Cards** cards for pleasure indicates that you will realize hopes and aspirations that have long sustained you. However, gambling for money may imply difficulties with friends. If you dream of losing at cards, you may encounter enemies, but winning is seen as an act of justifying yourself in the eyes of your peers. Each of the four suits is considered to have a specific meaning. Diamonds

represent success and wealth; Clubs indicate work and knowledge. Hearts are indicative of emotional affairs and personal relationships, while Spades signify obstacles that will take endurance and effort to overcome.

Carriages and Carts

Dreams of these old-fashioned modes of transport suggest the sleeper is unwilling to take risks in his or her waking life (or even in sleep). A carriage or cart without a horse foretells illness on a journey; to sit alone in one indicates that an impropriety or scandal is possibly about to overtake you.

Castles

The stronghold of a castle in a dream may either be interpreted as a good omen or a harbinger of bad luck. The dream's significance is determined by your own emotional response to the place – do its surrounding walls offer protection, or seem like a prison? If the latter is the case, it denotes that your hopes and desires are unlikely to be realized until you free yourself from the confines of outmoded and bigoted ideas. A drastic change may be indicated.

Cat

For such well-loved pets it is surprising to find that dreams about cats are almost universally regarded as omens of misfortune. Despite the well-known belief that a black cat crossing one's path brings

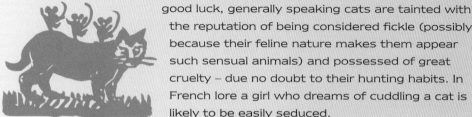

good luck, generally speaking cats are tainted with the reputation of being considered fickle (possibly because their feline nature makes them appear such sensual animals) and possessed of great cruelty – due no doubt to their hunting habits. In French lore a girl who dreams of cuddling a cat is likely to be easily seduced.

Caterpillars & Grubs

While dreams of butterflies are generally considered to be happy, those involving its larva-form are taken to be a sign that you will mix with uncouth and disreputable people who will cause you embarrassment, or try to drag you down to their level.

Chains

Chains are an unsettling subject to dream about, and an uneasy omen to decipher. They presage unjust burdens and impositions placed upon you, which can only be resolved by breaking the links. This could mean a change of job, or finding a new partner. Conversely, if you chain up someone else, this represents love combined with guilt and fear – a desire to possess those who would not otherwise stay with you.

Chalice

Indicative of female sexuality, the chalice is viewed in dream lore as "the well of the emotions." If it is seen to be overflowing, the dreamer is ruled by the heart, whereas an empty cup reflects a frigid disposition. The connection between chalice and grail can also endow this dream symbol with a spiritual dimension, whereby it represents the "fountain of life."

As you might expect, to see a chameleon in your

Chameleon

dreams suggests that you must adapt to the changing circumstances currently prevailing in your life. You must learn to "bend with the wind" a little more, and be less confrontational in your dealings with those around you (especially those who have authority over you) – adopt the camouflage of conformity, so you can influence decisions from within.

Cherries

The cherry is synonymous with voluptuous, lustful desire, due, no doubt, to the resemblance between the luscious fruit and seductive human lips. In dreams, to taste the flesh of a cherry symbolizes carnal desire, and it either bodes well or ill depending on whether the taste was sweet or sour. To dream of picking cherries portends you will be deceived in love.

The game of chess **Chess**
occurs quite frequently
in our dreamscapes, and when it
does it has a clear and precise
definition. To play the game, and
win, indicates a highly developed
and analytical mind which may,
unfortunately, be perceived by
others as dull or needlessly abrupt.
Losing at chess suggests that you
have been over-stretching your
talents, and you should lower your
expectations slightly. Perhaps this
will afford you the chance to
concentrate on personal matters –
which may have been neglected.

Chocolate

The sense of self-indulgence associated with buying, or eating, chocolate means that an element of puritanism can become evident when it is interpreted as a dream symbol. Perhaps it is outdated morality that nags the subconscious – anything which brings pleasure must be bad for you. Thus, in dreams, the taste of chocolate is thought to foretell a major item of expense and subsequent loss of money.

The squared-up conformity of the chess board (far left) and squares of chocolate (left) – in the symbolism of dreams both pastime and pleasure are very slightly frowned upon.

Church

A dream of a church may suggest that the individual's idealism is being repressed, giving rise to anxieties that are not apparent in waking life, but which express themselves in dreams. A church should be seen as a signal to acknowledge spiritual conflict, and seek to remedy it by adopting a more enlightened approach to life. The symbol of a church could also represent sanctuary – try to work out what you are running away from.

City

In the realms of sleep, a dream of a city is usually regarded as an omen of great success, but possibly at the expense of some aspect of your personal life – either an acrimonious split with a partner, or a legal dispute. To dream that you soar above a city and look down on it augurs well for financial investments, and implies that your ambitions, although high, will be realized. However, if no sign of life can be detected, the omens are reversed.

Climbing

Dreams of climbing are a metaphor for the personal ambitions of the sleeper. The climber struggles toward success, and the tougher the ascent, the harder the dreamer will have to strive to reach their goal. If progress is difficult and they slip, it probably indicates unrealistic ambitions which were set too high. To climb with a partner indicates the dreamer will have to rely on the support of a family member, or a close friend, if they are to overcome obstacles and reach the summit.

Clock

The symbol of a clock or watch appearing in your dreams may indicate that you are concerned with the minutiae of life, or are afraid you will not be able to face up to your responsibilities. To hear a clock ticking in a dream indicates a preoccupation with the passage of the years, and the fear that "time is running out." Similarly, to imagine winding a clock denotes anxiety that your days are finite – and you should make the most of every moment.

Clothes

Clothes reflect our personalities. They are the facade we choose to reveal to the world, and, as such, make interesting statements when encountered as dream symbols. To dress in smart and fashionable clothes indicates a slavish conformity – acting like a sheep, when you really want to be a wolf! This may explain why a dream of wearing dirty clothes is considered an omen of contentment. Similarly, to imagine wearing someone else's clothes indicates that you would like to be endowed with some of that person's attributes.

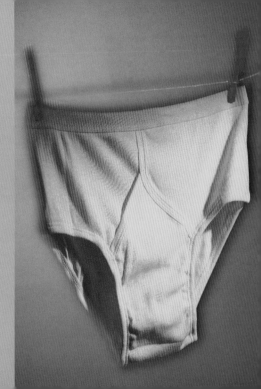

Fluffy white clouds are almost a dream cliché. In cartoons, they have come to represent the "thought-bubble."

Cloud

A dream of white clouds in a clear blue sky offers the prospect of advancement, and a chance meeting that could lead to romance. A grey blanket of clouds is not such an auspicious omen, as it foretells the dreamer may be creating a bad impression among those he or she needs to win over. Heavy, rain-laden clouds portend still worse – indicating a troubled period for the dreamer, but one that can be turned around by acting with a sense of duty and firm intent.

If a sleeper dreams of a # Coat of Arms
coat of arms, it probably
reflects their desire to rise above a perceived
station in life to enjoy a little of the cachet that
being ennobled would bring. The symbolism is a
representation of the desire to be accepted and
treated as an equal by those "above" you.

Coffin
Dreams of coffins rarely have
any associations with physical
death. Rather, they allude to the conclusion of a
situation, changes in feelings, or they signal that the
dreamer has moved on from one particular period of life to another. By
using such stark and uncompromising imagery, the subconscious serves
notice on the dreamer that the split is irrevocable – the old order is quite
literally "dead and buried."

Color

Colors tend to have an immediate impact upon our emotions, and our dreams reflect this. If an individual color predominates, its symbolism is usually significant:

Red – indicates a warning, anger, or sexual energy.

Yellow – pale tones imply health; darker hues, betrayal.

Blue – the color of spirituality, indiscretion, and the intellect.

Green – implies regrowth, but can also indicate jealousy.

Purple – a regal color denoting strength of character.

Gold – wealth and majesty, but, by extension, envy

Silver – the color of chastity and feminine spirituality.

White – symbolizes purity, virtue, and the transcendent.

Black – a harbinger of sorrow and a symbol of death.

Compass

Predicatably, a dream of a compass is your unconscious mind's way of graphically illustrating the need for "direction" in your life, or perhaps a change in its course. If you can remember which way the needle points, it may aid interpretation. The East symbolizes birth and earthly life; the South denotes warmth and passion; the West implies sunset and spiritual rebirth; while the North points to the shadowed realms of the spirit.

Computer

In a dream, the unconscious mind utilizes any object from which it feels able to derive symbolism and meaning. Thus, a dream of a computer suggests the sleeper needs to work out a complicated problem logically. If you are unsure of how the computer functions, or feel uncomfortable with the technology, it may indicate a project that seems overwhelming.

"If there were dreams to sell,
What would you buy?
Some cost a passing bell;
Some a light sigh,
That shakes from Life's
fresh crown
Only a roseleaf down.
If there were dreams to sell,
Merry and sad to tell,
And the crier rung the bell,
What would you buy?"

THOMAS LOVELL BEDDOES 1803–49

Countryside

To dream of living in the heart of the country, with fields set amid a well-wooded landscape, may indicate a desire for the solace of a little comfort and serenity within the turmoil of your current life. If the countryside is viewed in winter, barren and without foliage, it presages a period of greyness that offers little in the way of encouragement – a similar scene viewed at night portends melancholy.

Visions of a lush summer's landscape (left) bode well for the dreamer, promising a future of prosperity and contentment.

Courtship

Courtship, and the paths to romance, frequently appear in dreamscapes, but the omens are notoriously ambiguous to divine. A dream that you court a stunningly beautiful, or attractive, partner may foretell glittering prizes or, alternatively, disappointment due to excessive or unrealistic expectations. Dreamers who pursue a reluctant lover are seen to possess a tenacity to overcome obstacles placed in their path. If you imagine you have a rival for love, this indicates that you will be slow to assert yourself, and could lose favor due to indecision.

Crab

The crab's impenetrable shell and formidable pincers find echoes in our dreams, instructing us to be wary of those who achieve their goals by threats and bluster. Avoid dealing with such people, as their fiery tempers and ill disposition will exploit your vulnerability and grind down your resolution.

Creatures of guile and secrecy – both crab and crocodile have the power to haunt our darkest dreams. The first is seen as a warning of devious maneuvering, while the latter portends hidden menace.

Crocodile

By common consent, these reptiles represent the primeval forces of nature – red in tooth and claw. They symbolize hidden enemies, and dreams involving them seldom give comfort. They usually serve to caution the dreamer against the deception of supposed friends. Heed the warning when omens of this nature appear, for there are those who would gladly crush you if it advanced their own cause.

Crow

The crow's scavenging habits, ungainly demeanor, and deathly-black plumage have made the bird a dream-symbol almost wholly associated with misfortune. To hear its unpleasant cawing in your sleep is taken as an omen of bad luck. If, however, you have the presence of mind to turn away from the crow, or to curse its name, it is thought to reverse the omens and remove their negative associations.

Crowds

You may either feel at home in a crowd, or become alarmed by the sea of unknown faces. If you identify with the former emotion, to dream of a crowd is likely to indicate a desire not to be singled out – to avoid personal responsibilities and to become anonymous within its mass. Indeed, the crowd may be conjured up by your dream for the sole purpose of camouflaging you, who would otherwise stand out disconcertingly. Alternatively, to feel uncomfortable in a crowd may indicate concern about your appearance and the impression you make in public.

The old adage "you are never more alone than when you are in a crowd" is literally true for those who are terrified of being confronted by a seething mass of people. Unfortunately, such phobias all too readily influence our dreams.

Crown

A crown has two components. Its circular base represents perfection and the infinite, and its height indicates majesty. As a symbol encountered within dreams, it is usually considered to be a signal from your subconscious that it is time for you to stretch out to attain goals hitherto thought to be beyond your reach.

Cuckoo

The word "cuckold," signifying deception in marriage, derives from "cuckoo," a reflection of this bird's action in foisting its offspring upon unsuspecting foster parents. In similar vein, to dream of seeing a cuckoo implies problems between couples in a partnership; while to hear one presages a lack of understanding and jealousy within marriage.

The act of cutting or slashing with a sharp implement may **Cut** mean problems are brewing, a bad decision, or sad news concerning a loved one. To wound yourself by mistake in a dream does not bode well for the future, warning that actions you have recently taken will rebound against you.

The Gordian knot (shown right) was so ingeniously tied that no man could unfasten it. By simply cutting it with his sword, Alexander the Great supplied dreamers with a symbol that represents escape from difficult situations by one decisive action.

Dagger

If a dagger is seen in a dream it denotes vulnerability, perhaps to the attacks of those you perceive to be your enemies. If you manage to free the weapon from an assassin's grasp it is a sign that you will overcome misfortune. To stab another person signifies your own aggressive sexuality, but to wound yourself unintentionally may mean that you are being made aware of your own shortcomings.

Daisy

The simplest of country flowers. To dream of being in a meadow of wild daisies signifies contentment with life, and the assurance that the pursuit of pleasures, however humble, will lead to enrichment.

This is a common dream

Dance

subject and is usually a sign of youth, joyfulness, and vigor. It allows the body to follow its natural rhythms and express itself, putting the dreamer in touch with the "animal" in their soul. It may be seen as a prelude to, and a desire for, sexual activity. A lively dance may indicate that you should beware the outcome of a romance, and keep a watchful eye open for the threat of the unexpected.

Darkness

For a sleeper to dream of dark, shadowed realms may symbolize depression, or lack of direction. The dark and poisoned droplet that taints the chalice represents the dregs of a dreamer's psyche – perhaps an irrational phobia or shaming experience – which they seek to hide away. However, the dreamer's subconscious knows the location, and can find it at will.

If in your dreams you can manage to confront your "inner darkness," it is possible to envision moving toward the sunlight – as if emerging from a dark mist – where your problems can be exposed to the power of reason, and shown up as the imposters that they really are!

Daughter

The daughter of your dreamscape is likely to be the feminine aspect of "self," representing your "inner child." By observing your daughter's actions and emotions, you can gauge your own strengths and weaknesses. Her youth serves as your bulwark against the tide of change.

Dawn

In early Roman myth, dawn was personified as Aurora who rose from the sea in a horse-drawn chariot. In most cultures, as well as in dream lore, the rising Sun symbolizes hope and a new beginning. It predicts the dreamer's escape from current problems – to start afresh.

Death

Death occurs as a dream symbol quite regularly, and it is rarely (if ever) to be feared as a portent of ill omen. Such dreams may best be described as the slamming shut of a door – an event that marks the final closure of one particular way of being, and the birth of something new. Indeed, you should not discount the idea of the dreamer actually encouraging a vision of death so that, on waking, life appears all the sweeter.

Desert

The symbol of a desert is a recurring image in dreams, and foreshadows troubled times ahead. It is commonly held that if you dream of struggling across the vast, arid expanse of a desert, it indicates a desperate need to be loved and understood. To journey with a companion may suggest that there is an urgent need to repair the relationship. A dream of dying of thirst may indicate that you are experiencing difficulties coping with the stresses of life.

Dreams such as these invariably reflect and

Despair

magnify the vexations of everyday life. The theme of despair may result from stressful tension that builds up over the course of weeks or months – caused, perhaps, by an unwillingness to compromise on a matter of principle, a false accusation, or the continuous petty squabbles of home or office. Unlikely as it may appear, a dream of despair is often just the tonic that your mind needs to trigger the release of its well of frustrated and poisoned emotions.

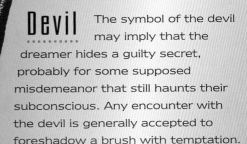

Devil

The symbol of the devil may imply that the dreamer hides a guilty secret, probably for some supposed misdemeanor that still haunts their subconscious. Any encounter with the devil is generally accepted to foreshadow a brush with temptation. In this respect, an argument might be made that he is a servant of God, in that he forewarns of and punishes sin.

The devil has always been regarded as the forerunner of despair (far left), and to dream of his presence is never a comfortable experience.

Diving

To dream that you are diving into clear water may be taken as a sign that once you have started on a venture, or a course of action, it is important to follow it through regardless of setbacks. If the water is cloudy or muddy, beware hidden pitfalls caused by overstretching your finances.

To encounter a doctor in a dream should be taken as a sign that you should visit the surgery

Doctor

if you have any health problems, however slight, that need attention. Take comfort, dream omens such as these invariably have a satisfactory outcome and set the mind at ease.

Dog

In dreams about humankind's best friend, the qualities of loyalty and determination feature prominently; they symbolize the dreamer's desire to balance their sense of loyalty with their needs for self-esteem and approval. Small dogs in a dream point to a frivolous nature; a large dog indicates that fidelity and courage bring their own rewards; whereas snarling, or barking, dogs simply mirror our own fears.

Dolphin

Despite the dolphin's associations in real life (its sense of fun and love of human company), a dream of a dolphin is thought to foretell anxiety, and the stagnation of ambition. They are considered to be unfavorable omens in dream lore, and to see one in your sleep, leaping in and out of the waves, serves as a caution to dreamers to beware that they do not misinterpret "bad judgment" for "good intent."

Dove

To dream of this worldwide symbol of humankind's desire for peace and spirituality indicates a striving for precisely those ideals. The dove is a harbinger that all is well with our world. To see one feeding from your hand should be taken as a sign that any worries that you may have are unfounded.

Dragon

With its breath of fire, wings to take to the air, scales of a water serpent, and dwelling deep within the caverns of the Earth, the dragon epitomizes the four elements, and unifies them in a single creature that has the power to inspire our imagination and haunt our nightmares. It is a paradox of good and evil, creativity and destruction. To dream of a dragon represents the life force, and the need of the dreamer to utilize this power to overcome fear.

Drink

Our sleeping minds may choose to alight upon this subject simply because we are thirsty. The dream's portent is dictated by the nature of the drink – is it wholesome and thirst-quenching, or is it drunk for excitement, or intoxication ? To drink clear water symbolizes rejuvenation, whereas to imagine you drink hot water signifies sickness. Not surprisingly, stagnant water, if drunk, indicates violent illness. To dream of swallowing cloudy liquid predicts losses; while beers and wines (when taken in moderation) indicate a need for discretion to avoid public criticism.

Drought

A dream that you are enduring a time of drought may symbolize a period somber with omens of misfortune. Work will prove a scourge for scant reward. The dreamer, however, can take solace, for this harrowing time will pass – leaving you wiser and better prepared for any further pitfalls that fate may cast in your way.

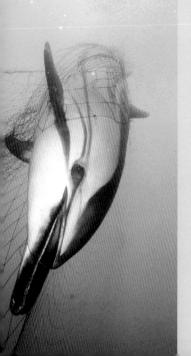

Drowning

The panic and suffocation of drowning may seem horribly real to the dreamer, and implies you are being overwhelmed by feelings that you cannot control. To save yourself, or be rescued, is a positive sign that indicates that, in waking life, you can rely upon your own resourcefulness, or the goodwill of friends.

Eagle

An eagle in a dream represents the qualities of strength and self-enlightenment. The bird points to the shedding of old worn-out ideas, and a freedom from earthly bounds. However, dreamers should examine their own desire for dominance, and the predatory motives of others.

The eagle
represents the
sky god – the nobility
of power that can soar
above the world of
humanity,
comprehending
and seeing all
things.

"*While men are dreaming they do not perceive that it is a dream. Some will even have a dream within a dream. And so when the great awakening comes upon us, shall we know this life to be a great dream. Fools believe themselves to be awake now!*"

CHINESE SAGE

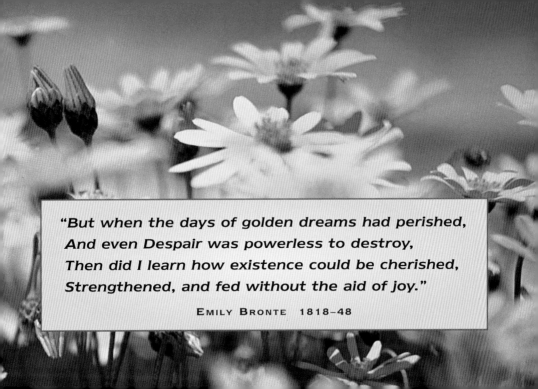

"But when the days of golden dreams had perished,
And even Despair was powerless to destroy,
Then did I learn how existence could be cherished,
Strengthened, and fed without the aid of joy."

EMILY BRONTE   1818–48

Ear A dream in which an ear features is usually concerned with the gossip and rumor that surround us. It indicates the need for the dreamer to listen carefully to what is said in the dream, as it might well presage exciting news. Any loss of hearing, however, could portend trouble from an unexpected source.

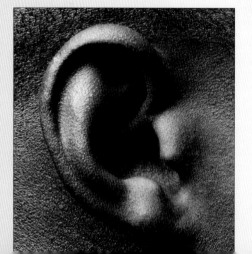

This element is **Earth** associated with the solid, practical side of our nature. To dream of sandy soil denotes uncertainties; red earth reflects shyness; and dark soil indicates luck and prosperity. If you see yourself digging in the earth this is a sign of great contentment – both physically and spiritually.

Parched earth is an ill-omen. Its arid desolation mirrors inner conflict. Look for any signs of hope – emergent growth, or the first spots of rain.

Sometimes the interpretation of # Eclipse dream symbols can seem irrational or elusive, while others seem to offer up an obvious meaning immediately. A dream about an eclipse falls into the latter category and, quite literally, indicates that a shadow is about to be cast over the dreamer's life. It might symbolize feelings of rejection at work – of being overshadowed somehow – or it could reflect personal worries about falling foul of the law and besmirching your honor.

Eggs

These point to creative inspiration, and symbolize a longing to conceive. In the teachings of alchemy, the inner man emerges complete and perfect from the egg (where the light of reason penetrates darkness), and this may be seen by the dreamer as a metaphor for searching out the artistic and creative talents that lie dormant within them, awaiting expression. However, beware of "feeling feathers before the egg is cracked" – as patience is always required to avoid unnecessary and hasty mistakes.

Elephant

In dreams, the elephant represents foresight and strength. Its longevity is generally supposed to stand for dignity in old age, and ultimate victory over death. As an image encountered during sleep, it is regarded as a lucky omen of success in business affairs and denotes prosperity. To dream of feeding an elephant indicates you will elevate your standing within the community by your acts of kindness.

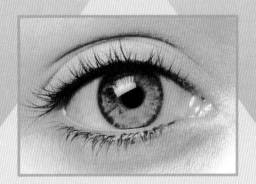

Eye

Symbolically, the eye represents the human psyche, " the window of the soul." It can be seen on dollar bills (a reminder of its mystical symbolism), as well as within the realms of sleep – where its appearance is generally taken to be a talisman of good fortune.

Fairy

Fairytales and children's books tend to ignore the malevolent personalities that these nature sprites were once thought to possess. In dreams, old beliefs are harder to dispel, and fairies remain untrustworthy beings despite their beguiling appearance. What seems to be passing pleasure signifies trouble; this trait is underlined by their favorite nighttime trick of using gold to entice mortals away from home – the treasure reverts to the dead leaves of human vanity with the dawn.

Fall

Keats' *"season of mists and mellow fruitfulness"* conjures up a sense of poetry even in its dream significance. Summer's richness draws to a slow end, ushering in the Fall to symbolize "harvest" and a gradual winding-down to the solace of rest. Its implication for the dreamer is to reap what has been sown before it is too late.

Falling

Falling, or the accompanying sensation of vertigo, is one of the most frequently experienced dreams. It occurs in virtually all cultures throughout the world, and is symbolic of a basic struggle occurring in the dreamer's life.

In dreams, the sensation of falling can encompass various anxieties – from the insecurity of business dealings to sexual feelings of inadequacy. Such may be the terror that the sleeper may wake in alarm. Should this occur, try to remember the circumstances of how and why you fell, as these may throw light upon the dream's inner meaning.

In another context, a dream of falling could signify that the dreamer is yielding to sexual or romantic temptation, and is literally "falling in love." Curiously, the longer the fall, the sooner the romance will be over.

Father and Mother

If you dream of your parents, it reveals a desire on your part for security and approval – especially if you imagine yourself to be a child again. Childhood is the time when the basic pattern from which all future relationships develop. Parents play a major role in dreamscapes, and nearly always represent themselves (or an archetype they have helped mold). So the symbolism of a mother or a father will mean different things to different dreamers, and defies generalized interpretation. One common trait, however, is their appearance (as in life) to express support or disapproval of your actions – this arouses powerful emotions even if you are an adult with children of your own!

Fear and Terror

Fear, as an emotional response unrelieved by the workings of the intellect, is as old as humankind. Thus nightmares are able to assume terrifying magnitude. Although distressing for the dreamer, modern psychologists believe that it is a healthy sign if deep-seated fears are aroused in sleep. It shows the subconscious mind's desire to face up to problems that are conveniently avoided when awake – by releasing this tension we unburden ourselves.

Fear of predatory evil stimulated our primitive ancestors to make the critical choice of "fight or flight" – "kill or be killed." By taking appropriate action our survival as a species was ensured, but with it came emotional turmoil that many dreamers wish they could avoid.

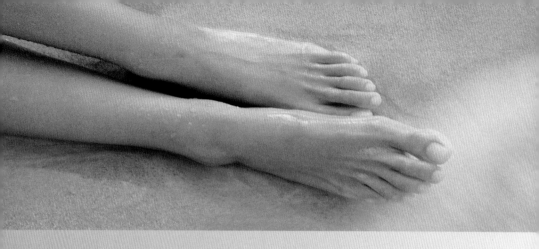

Feet

Feet are our foundation and the basis of stability in life; to dream of them represents fundamental issues. They can symbolize a desire to "find our feet" and make the most of whatever opportunities present themselves or, alternatively, they may caution dreamers to watch where bad habits are leading them.

Fence

Fences are man-made structures that impose order upon wild nature. They symbolize self-control, and pent-up emotion. Fences also express the dreamer's feelings about being enclosed – either as a plea for greater privacy, or a desire to break down the barriers that restrict personal freedom.

A subconscious mind may resort to the image of "sitting on the fence" to reveal its disquiet over a lack of moral courage or an inability to come to a firm decision.

Fields

In the realms of dreams, fields are interpreted as symbols denoting contentment and a "sense of place." Their green pastures evoke a feeling of belonging and spiritual ease. If the fields are seen to be ripe with corn or grain, this presages great happiness; ploughed fields indicate future honor; but those fields left untended, or with shriveled crops, are considered to be an unfavorable omen.

To become involved in a **Fight** fight suggests physical confidence. The way dreamers feel about the circumstances of the fight will be determined by their combative spirit. However, the omens surrounding the symbolism of fighting are seldom favorable, and usually foretell a loss of prestige. To dream that you fight and win may symbolize a successful lawsuit, or landing a prestigious contract, but it also carries the implicit warnings against pride and arrogance. To lose a fight indicates loss of face and a lack of conviction.

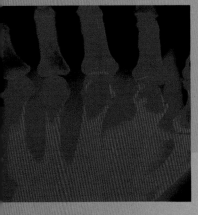

Fingers

Fingers often feature in our dreams, where they are linked to expression, dexterity, and the sensuality of touch. Pointed fingers imply a guilty conscience, and dirty nails foretell a life of toil and hardship. However, to dream of wearing rings augurs well for future happiness – in which hope is realized and endeavor rewarded.

Fire

Fire is one of the four dream elements and symbolizes energy, brilliance, and the passion of the emotions. Those who frequently dream of fire usually suffer from a quick temper, and would benefit from greater self-control and temperance. During illness, you may dream of trying to stamp out a fire that has been raging out of control; this is a good omen as it indicates you are well on the way to recovery.

Firmament

When the firmament – the celestial vault of heaven – is seen in a dream it can bode for good or ill. If it is seen to be flecked with red, or golden, cloud, this implies atonement and a calm spirit. However, if you see the firmament in turmoil – racked by wild winds and raging storms – it forewarns against an introverted personality which will ensnare you by your own phobic reactions.

Fish

In may cultures fish are regarded as symbols of fecundity, and their lives spent in the depths (deep water is held to represent unconscious thought) make them dream omens of creativity and inspiration. To see a fish swimming in clear water is an indication that you possess latent spiritual insight. To dream of a fish's eye indicates diligence and watchfulness; however, a dead fish signifies an inability to relate to others, due to a lack of emotional warmth.

Flag

Dreams in which you see your national flag are commonly interpreted as omens of good fortune during periods of war; in peace they imply success in personal ventures. Red banners (not unnaturally) warn against danger – possibly a threat to a friend who will seek your help. More recently, foreign flags have come to be regarded as symbolic of travel, and if you can identify the country to which your dream flag belongs, it may be worth considering a trip there on vacation.

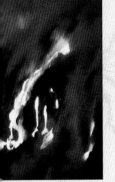

Flame

If the emphasis of the dream is more on light shed than on heat radiated, a solitary flame can represent the focus of the inner spirit – a reflection of grace. To dream that you are encircled by flame denotes a creative, inventive, or artistic nature that is currently dormant, but which yearns for outlet and expression.

Flies

Beelzebub is styled "Lord of the Flies," and associations with the Devil make these detested insects a dream symbol of sickness and contagion (a medical examination could even be forecast). Swarms of flies may appear a petty annoyance, but they serve to alert the dreamer to enemies who individually pose no threat, but, if united, could cause great trouble.

Flowers

Flowers startle our dullness, and remind us of the beauty and resonant melodies of nature. Ancient peoples perceived paradise filled with blossom, and imagined that for each woman living in the world, a flower bloomed in the next. These beliefs are mirrored in dreams, where flowers have come to symbolize female beauty and the joy of the spirit. To dream of a flower bud opening represents creation – the blossoming of the individual, often through a new relationship involving tenderness and love. Flowers are symbols of youth and vitality but, because of their impermanence and fragility, they caution the dreamer against the self-deceit of vanity.

To see ripe seed heads augurs well for the dreamer as they denote the correct and natural order of things – events are progressing according to plan.

Flying

This is one of the most common of all dreams, and conjures up the fantasy of flying confidently over a panoramic landscape below. Indeed, some people believe that such dreams are not "true" dreams at all, but "astral projection" – occasions when the spirit temporarily leaves the physical body.

For sleepers to dream that they are flying should be regarded as a positive sign, as it represents the subconscious mind's way of registering your confidence and contentment – as well as symbolizing a yearning for spiritual and intellectual ascent. The sensation of flying can be intensely sensual (Freud declared the whole dream purely sexual), and may signify a desire to enjoy a greater degree of intimacy with a partner, and a willingness to explore different avenues toward that goal.

Forest

Dreaming of wandering in a dense forest indicates a risky enterprise, or is symbolic of the dreamer's failure to find a satisfactory path in life. It highlights a need for clarity and guidance – metaphorically the dreamer "cannot see the wood for the trees." If the forest is particularly dark and deep, this may be a deliberate image created by the subconscious to symbolize the "shadow side" of the dreamer's psyche. To travel through the forest and reach the other side is a favorable omen.

Forest Fire

Unlikely as it may appear, most
authorities on dreams agree that
to see a forest on fire in your
dreams is a positive symbol that
bodes well for the sleeper. It may
echo events in nature, where the
scourging flame is intermittently
necessary to encourage new
growth. To hide in a forest suggests
a guilty secret, but a forest laid bare
by fire offers little shelter. Thus the
dreamer is compelled to confront their
problems in the open, and hopefully
overcome them.

Fortune Telling

If you have your fortune told in a dream, it is probable that uncertainties lie ahead. Resorting to acts of divination indicates you have important decisions to make. Your subconscious reflects this anxiety and asks you to seek a solution from someone you know and trust – although this is unlikely to be a fortune-teller!

Fox

Foxes symbolize trouble. They are creatures of wily habit, who can blend into their surroundings to observe others unnoticed. In dreams, these aspects of the fox's sly character are transferred to a rival, who should be watched carefully in case he or she causes mischief.

Some dreams are experienced in a

Freedom

wonderfully relaxed spirit. Perhaps you imagine a carefree childhood day, running free on a beach, or a similarly uplifting dreamscape. However, this freedom is probably your subconscious compensating for a feeling of being trapped in waking life. Try to recapture some of the fun that gave you such pleasure in earlier life.

To see a fox (left) warns against deceitful rivals. In the West the creature is considered an unfortunate omen of cunning, but in Oriental mythology it is seen as a lucky talisman, representing longevity and enlightenment.

"What is life? A frenzy. What is life?
An illusion, a shadow, a fiction.
And the greatest good is of slight worth,
as all life is a dream,
and dreams are dreams."

PEDRO CALDERÓN DE LA BARCA   1600–81

"All that we see or seem is but a dream within a dream."

EDGAR ALLEN POE 1809–49

Friend

Perhaps the most common example of predictive dreams are those in which we dream of friends – who may have moved a long distance away, or from whom we have not heard for a long time – and the next morning a letter or telephone call from them comes out of the blue. Chance and coincidence probably pay a role, but such occasions serve to underline the close bonds of emotions that link friends, even in their dreams!

Fright

Dreams in which you confront your worst fears dredge the depths of humanity's elemental emotions. They can cause the sleeper much turmoil, but, be assured, it is better for your subconscious to bring these feelings to the surface than to let them fester unaddressed.

In dreams fright can be the shock tactic your mind uses to focus on phobias – only by confronting your worst fears can they eventually be conquered.

Frogs and Toads

Once regarded as representing the repulsive side of life, frogs and toads (and also serpents) are now seen to denote wisdom and the power to see the sacred in all things. They presage a period of transformation, and tell dreamers to find some time in their busy lives to do whatever they feel is needed to refresh and replenish themselves.

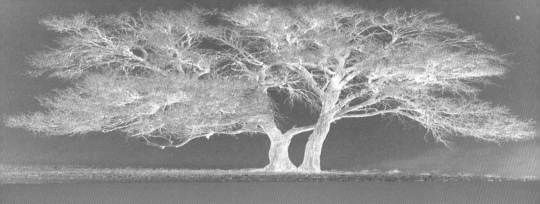

Frost

Dreams in which frost appears suggest that a fresh start is needed in some area of your life. If you notice that the landscape seems magically transformed – perhaps the trees and bushes are silvered with rime and sparkle in the sunlight – it indicates that you will shortly travel to an exotic location that, hitherto, you knew little about. An overnight hoar-frost that kills emergent Spring foliage cautions the dreamer to beware of assuming success before it is truly earned.

Fruit

To dream of fruit can have sexual connotations and the symbol of a bowl of ripe fruit may indicate the hungry libido of the dreamer. Eating fresh fruit in your dreams denotes a healthy sexual appetite; but unripe or rotting fruit may presage a frigid nature. Fruit might also foretell a pregnancy – after the flower (the flame of love) comes the fruit!

Frustration

If you experience a dream in which you appear to meet with frustration at every turn, this probably echoes your working life – where you might experience unrealistic deadlines, canceled orders, or the feeling that bureaucracy delights in tying you up in red-tape. Such dreams can, however, act as safety valves, and are a method by which the subconscious mind rids itself of frustration – that parasitic emotion that feeds on stress and misery.

Gallows

The vision of a gallows, scaffold, or any other instrument of capital punishment in your dreams could indicate that your subconscious is seeking to warn you to avoid the trap of being self-righteous, or overcritical of others. However, if the dreamer realizes that it is they who are to be executed, it implies a guilty secret which cannot be hidden.

Gambling

To dream that you gamble and win is seldom, if ever, a sign to risk money on a wager. Rather, it is likely to foretell the "correct result," or desired outcome, of a situation that has hitherto been troubling you. A dream of losing a wager should be heeded as a warning against taking unnecessary risks in your financial, or personal, life.

Garden

A well-kept garden full of bright blooms and foliage portends great happiness and abundant love. Often it signifies that the unconscious mind is reflecting back to early childhood when our first visions of the wide world took place within the protective security of flower-covered walls and fences. Abandoned or overgrown gardens are omens that difficulties may lie ahead.

In dream lore gardens are thought to possess feminine qualities. Nothing exemplifies this better than Samuel Palmer's visionary homage to Springtide fecundity "In a Shoreham Garden."

Gargoyle

These peculiar creatures of the Medieval mind were originally sculpted to adorn the walls of churches and cathedrals on the premise that evil can be used to drive away evil. Thus the more demonic and hideous they may seem, the greater is their power to protect. To dream of a gargoyle indicates that we should guard against taking people at face-value. The true worth of a person lies within his or her being, and is not merely to be judged by the face that he or she chooses to display to the world. Guard against duplicity and select your friends carefully.

Gate

For a dreamer to see an open gate indicates that opportunities lie ahead that may usher in beneficial changes – but these will only be won by firm resolve and determination. If the gate remains shut in the dream, it augurs less well and can indicate various minor difficulties that stand between you and a close acquaintance.

Ghost

You should never be afraid of a ghost in your dream. It may represent a message from your "spirit" (soul), and you should try to act upon any advice that may be offered. Ghosts are viewed as bringers of consolation, and among the most comforting and cherished visions are those in which a father or mother returns to the dreamscape of the sleeper.

Giant

An encounter with a giant in your dreams can presage an uphill struggle against the odds – the larger the giant, the greater the endeavor. The dream's symbolism also links the giant's size to that of other larger-than-life persons (parents seem enormous to small children), and so reveals the dreamer's lack of self-confidence.

Gifts

If you dream of receiving a gift at the start of a new romance, it portends that love will be reciprocated. However, the receipt of a gift should seldom be welcomed in a dream, as it usually implies trickery and an attempt to deceive.

God

In the realms of sleep, a dream that you have personal contact with the Creator may be your subconscious mind's way of trying to jolt you into respecting the needs of your inner spirit. Whatever your religious beliefs (or lack of them), a dream about God seeks to reintroduce you to certain fundamental "truths" that may be vital to your welfare, and helps guide you to deeper wisdom and understanding.

God's presence in a dream should always be seen as a positive omen (despite any rebukes, or criticism, offered), and any message relayed in your dream is likely to be significant – a catalyst for spiritual advance, rather than the atrophy which currently stifles your life.

Golf

A dream that you are playing a round of golf on your own may signify feelings of resentment that you have been left alone to cope. To play with agreeable companions augurs well for business dealings; but if you record a poor score, this should alert you to the possibility that malicious and untrustworthy friends will offer bad advice, and seek to influence others against you.

Gossip

Dreaming that other people are talking about you behind your back reflects the common concern that, in waking life, you are undervalued and overlooked. However, if the dreamer is the person spreading gossip, it indicates that they are aware of an aspect of their own personality that would not stand up to close scrutiny.

Grapes

Dreams in which you eat grapes signify profit and cheerfulness; to see them hanging in rich profusion from the vine may be taken as a talisman promising promotion and a bright future. If the grapes appear lustrous, but are sour to the taste, this indicates that you have the fervent desire to make money, but a strong disinclination to spend it.

Grass

Green, healthy grass should always be interpreted as a fortunate omen presaging affluence and plenty. It may seem an unlikely topic to feature in dreams, but it harks back to an age when grass was vital to our farming ancestors – insufficient winter fodder meant starvation for both human and beast. To view brown and withered grass indicates exhaustive effort for scant reward.

Grave

A dream featuring a grave is an obvious allusion to mortality, and can be a warning from your subconscious mind to look after your health. If you dream of attending a burial, you probably regret some past action involving that person, and are being shown the necessity of coming to terms with the transgression. The unsettling vision of your own grave signifies overwhelming current difficulties – troubles that you fear you may never be able to "dig your way out of."

Gun

Guns are an unfavorable dream omen, denoting "trouble today and trouble tomorrow." To a certain extent, their shape and function mirror the phallus and thus handling a weapon in your dreams serves to emphasize the base link between violent aggression and sexuality. If you dream that you have been shot, every effort should be made in waking life to handle weapons with caution. These efforts must be redoubled if you dream that you shoot another person – a vision that hints at possible trouble in the coming weeks.

Gymnast

A dream in which you appear as a gymnast reveals a desire for greater self-expression than your lifestyle currently permits. Your subconscious mind may be urging you to stretch yourself more, but a balance must be reached between what are achievable ambitions, and what are unattainable goals.

Hammer

The appearance of a hammer in a dream emphasizes the urgency of a message we are trying to communicate to others by figuratively "hammering home the point." The louder the clang of metal – the more emphatic we are seen to become! If a dream involves a hammer and nails, it forebodes much toil for small reward, but

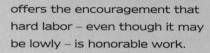

offers the encouragement that hard labor – even though it may be lowly – is honorable work.

In Norse mythology, as Thor, the God of Thunder, rode across the sky, he threw down his hammer to produce thunderbolts. So in early dream lore a vision of a hammer was believed to be a talisman protecting your home from fire.

Hand

Hands possess an elegance that expresses certain emotions in a way that words seldom can. Thus, few images could equal that of a baby's hand to represent purity and future promise. Similarly, creativity, contact, and practical application are all symbolized in dreams by images of hands.

Dreams of hairy hands (rather incongruously) point to the possibility of imprisonment; dirty or bloodied hands indicate looming problems; washing your hands suggests the need to rectify a misdemeanor, or be rid of a past embarrassment.

Hawk

If the symbol of a hawk appears in your dreams, it is a message to be on your guard for hazards – especially in your personal life. The bird indicates a need to keep a strong watchful eye on matters relating to romance, for you have a rival, and they are ready to pounce upon your slightest mistake.

Head

The brain – its intellect and logic – is symbolized in dreams by the head. So if you imagine a headache in your dreams, it is probably a plea to stop worrying. It carries the implied message to be happy by learning to find pleasure in the worth of simple things.

Heart

Over the centuries the heart has been viewed as the universal symbol of love, intuition, and compassion. It also stands for the center of things – the heart of the matter. Thus, in dream lore this symbol is highly regarded as an omen, and it is capable of indicating either excitement and joy, or self-pity and sadness. The heart's most common association is with romance, and if a dreamer imagines any heart-shaped object it presages a love affair. However, a dream that you see a living, beating heart forewarns that you will suffer from lack of energy.

Heaven

No two people's images of heaven are ever the same. Each brings their own ideals of perfection, yet, by the common consent of most cultures, it is usually accepted that heaven is found above the Earth – in the realms of the sky or, more recently, space. Indeed, the words "heaven" and "the heavens" are similar in meaning in almost all languages.

To dream of this ethereal world usually entails an awareness of traveling to a spiritual dimension, and may involve the dreamer in a form of astral projection (an out-of-body experience). Ultimately, this is a life-enriching experience which, if nurtured, can cleanse away earthly problems and anxieties.

Hell

Unlikely to be high on any dreamer's list of favorite destinations, the Medieval image of hell lingers still, and has the power to terrify even the most skeptical minds. As you might expect, a vision of hell is considered an ill omen. To descend into its fiery depths is a warning to guard against temptations that may damage you physically and morally.

To dream of visiting hell – to smell the brimstone, burn in the flame, and know the lamentations of the damned – suggests a period of melancholic reflection. It indicates that you may fall foul of an enemy with a fiery temper.

The medical and culinary value of herbs have been appreciated throughout the ages. Their symbolism carries rich significance in the realms of our dreams.

Herbs

In general, dreams relating to herbs are considered fortunate and symbolize stability and peace of mind. If however, the dream is associated with illness, your subconscious may be prompting you to consider the use of alternative medicine, if conventional medication is proving ineffective.

Over the centuries, symbolic meaning has become attached to the particular properties of individual herbs. Rue reflects the bitterness of sorrow and repentance, rosemary holds a scent which lingers like a fond memory, thyme is seen as an omen of "love-forsaken," and marjoram is thought to absolve and purify.

Hops

Few plants have a greater aura of mystery than the hop. A dream of them foretells the gift of prophesy, and an ability to understand the hidden workings of the natural world. At the height of harvest, hops (which are used to clarify and flavor beer) hang in aromatic cones from the bine and they can be used to make hop pillows. These are valued as a natural aid to counter insomnia and help induce sweet dreams.

To dream of picking hops denotes confidence in business ventures, stemming from your power to grasp and master innovative ideas and inventive propositions.

Horse

The presence of this magnificent animal in a dream serves to remind sleepers of the latent power of their own bodies. Horse dreams are essentially about energy, and how we chose to channel it in the pursuit of our ambitions. To envision riding a horse, especially a white one, points to a contented life with good prospects. Horses running free foretell a passionate love affair; while if a woman dreams of riding bareback, it indicates the desire to be seduced by an ardent lover. However, to be thrown from a horse is to be spurned in love.

Horseshoe

This is an ancient symbol of the Moon goddess, and a classic good-luck charm (when seen with the opening uppermost). It is an excellent talisman to dream of finding a horseshoe, foretelling a charmed existence. If you imagine picking one up from the road, this indicates success in the face of pessimism; however, a broken shoe is considered to indicate ill-luck.

Gambling dreams are seldom accurate – we only every hear about winners, never the vast majority of dreamers whose "visions" lose! Never gamble more on horses than you can comfortably afford to lose.

"I dreamed that, as I wandered by the way,
Bare Winter suddenly was changed to Spring,
And gentle odours led my steps astray,
Mixed with a sound of water's murmuring
Along a shelving bank of turf, which lay
Under a copse, and hardly dared to fling
Its green arms round the bosom of the stream,
But kissed it and then fled, as thou mightst in
dream."

PERCY BYSSHE SHELLEY 1792–1822

Hospital

Dreamers invariably feeel anxious about such dreams, as they interpret them as a precognition dream indicating that the dreamer, or someone who is close to them, will face a traumatic time in hospital. Rest assured, this is seldom, if ever, the case! The commonly accepted interpretation of dreams relating to becoming a patient, or visiting a hospital, is that your subconscious is warning you to beware of worrying too much, or overworking. The dreamer's equanimity and ability to cope are being placed under pressure. You need to talk things through with a sympathetic friend, who can help to lift the load and make things better. A further element of the dream interpretation may reflect a degree of phobia about illness – where the dreamer fears being hospitalized.

House

The words "house" and "home" are virtually interchangeable; and as dream symbols they follow a parallel path. The house (home) is the center of most people's lives, and to dream of it is usually a favorable omen. As in waking life, however, niggling faults or minor problems about the home can filter through to the subconscious, to be replayed as symbols. Thus, a damaged lock, or broken blind, may highlight the dreamer's vulnerability, or lack of privacy. A poorly maintained house indicates the need to repair a rift; whereas to dream about your childhood home may be interpreted as a regressive fantasy as you seek to evade current problems.

A family argument may prompt your subconscious into employing extreme symbols. To see your home destroyed by fire places squabbles into a proper perspective.

Hunger

A dream of hunger is one of contradiction. It is a classic example of a symbol signifying the exact opposite of what one might expect. Paradoxically, the greater your hunger in a dream, the more fortune is likely to reward you.

Hunt

To dream of hunting a wild animal denotes intrigue involving a loved one. If you are the hunted victim, however, it could mean that toil and tribulation are beginning to grind away and wear you down.

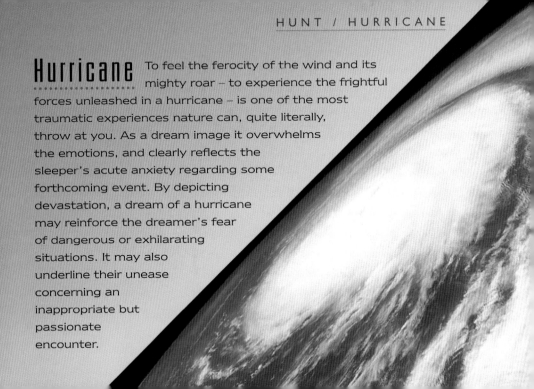

Hurricane

To feel the ferocity of the wind and its mighty roar – to experience the frightful forces unleashed in a hurricane – is one of the most traumatic experiences nature can, quite literally, throw at you. As a dream image it overwhelms the emotions, and clearly reflects the sleeper's acute anxiety regarding some forthcoming event. By depicting devastation, a dream of a hurricane may reinforce the dreamer's fear of dangerous or exhilarating situations. It may also underline their unease concerning an inappropriate but passionate encounter.

Ice

In human perception, and in nature, ice symbolizes coldness and rigidity. Its melting is, therefore, a welcome herald of renewed life. To dream of ice in Winter has no particular symbolic meaning, but in any other season it denotes a frozen heart that is closed to the warmth of love. To slip or slide on ice foretells an unprofitable enterprise, and to see a thin sheet of ice implies a promise which, like the ice, will be easily broken.

Ice Cream

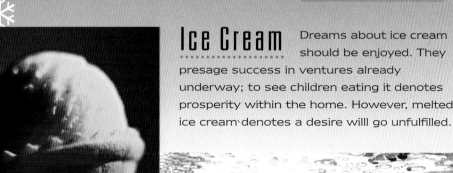

Dreams about ice cream should be enjoyed. They presage success in ventures already underway; to see children eating it denotes prosperity within the home. However, melted ice cream denotes a desire willl go unfulfilled.

Icicles

In the realms of dreams, icicles are regarded as symbols indicating that those who have acted coldly toward you in the past will change their attitudes and try to develop a warmer relationship. Your anxieties and doubts about them will melt away. If dreamers see icicles hanging from their homes, it indicates that they will find common ground with a past rival, and a friendship may ensue.

To dream of icicles lit by the Sun and thawing can indicate the conquest in love of one who has hitherto rejected your advances.

Illness and Injury

Pain and sickness are never welcome. To encounter them in a dream rarely indicates actual physical illness, or injury, in the waking world. If the dreamer imagines a specific illness, it might be wise to consult a doctor – if only to set your mind at rest! It is far more likely, however, that the dream is your subconscious mind's way of sending coded warnings that it is unhappy with some aspect of your health. Perhaps you smoke or drink too heavily, or do not eat healthily, and have closed your mind to the risks and unpalatable consequences. An illness dream is your subconscious "pleading" with you to win back your future.

Insects

To imagine you see insects in your dreams could indicate you have many small irritations in your waking life. You may wish to be rid of these vexations, but seem powerless to deal with them. A swarm of insects is often a sign that you are feeling restricted because other people are putting pressure on you to conform. This is stifling your creativity – don't let your neighbors set your standards; be yourself.

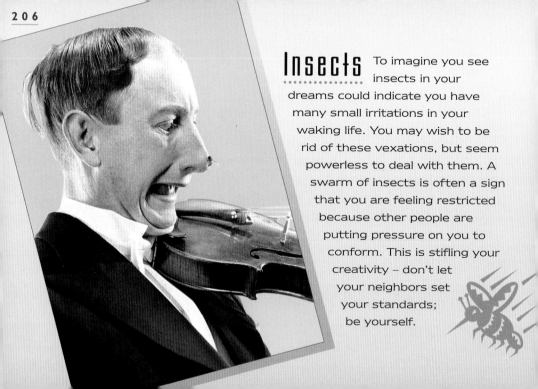

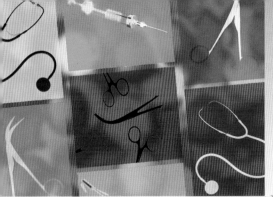

Instruments

In general, to dream of musical instruments implies the anticipation of pleasure, whereas surgical instruments denote a general caution – particularly in relation to your health.

Medical instruments (above), such as a scalpel or a stethoscope, act as omens to warn the sleeper to beware of taking unnecessary risks with their health. Musical instruments (right) generally signify more welcome omens of benevolence and spiritual sustenance.

A dream about being an inventor is one of aspiration, of striving to achieve high ideals. There may also be a suggestion of seeking the approval of others by your scientific prowess, and of creating something worthwhile for the benefit of all humankind. Unfortunately, research has found that few dreamers can remember details of their "great invention" on waking – let alone profit from their original idea.

Inventor

Invisible

To dream of being invisible may indicate how you feel in everyday life – unnoticed by those around you. The dream's symbolism may indicate you feel ashamed of some vulnerable area of your life that you would prefer to keep hidden away. An element of voyeurism adds piquancy to the dream, but expect to discover some unpleasant home-truths about yourself.

Jail

Dreams of imprisonment can symbolize feelings of entrapment – where you are committed to a course of action that you know will upset those dear to you. Alternatively, you could be "locking away" some aspect of your psyche about which you feel unhappy, or you wish to punish.

Jealousy

Many commentators maintain that to dream about jealousy is a sign of ill-omen, denoting a split in a partnership or the termination of a long-standing romance. However, it is just as probable that the emotion reflects the dreamer's own feelings of insecurity when faced with separation and loss.

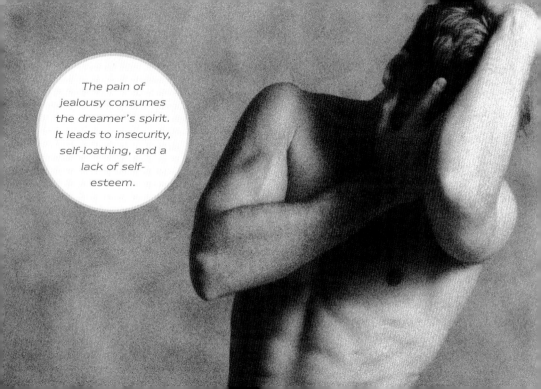

The pain of jealousy consumes the dreamer's spirit. It leads to insecurity, self-loathing, and a lack of self-esteem.

Journey and Travel

Dreams involving travel and journeys are a long-established theme, and invariably symbolize the individual's "way" through life. By rail or road, through the sky or upon the oceans – the dream always represents destiny. Whether this path-through-life is traveled with ease, or is an uphill struggle, depends upon the nature of the journey. If the experience is pleasant, it augurs achievement and good health; but if you dream that you travel on foot, this indicates hard slog for scant reward. The faster the transport the subconscious selects, the quicker dreamers will accomplish their ambitions.

Dreams of travel can encompass any destination, from the mundane to the miraculous. Our subconscious minds can transport us from the station platform to the far depths of the galaxy (left). Whatever destination is reached, our dreams will have significance – as they indicate the point along life's journey that the dreamer has currently reached.

Kettle

The kettle has been a symbol of hearth and home for centuries. To dream that you wait for one to boil could reflect your own impatience, and desire for events to reach a swift conclusion. If you dream that a kettle is boiling over, it may symbolize your current mood – steamed-up and about to explode! Similarly, a broken kettle, or one that has boiled dry, may mirror the dreamer's own feelings of emptiness – as though the very life-force has been drained from within them.

Freud viewed the key as a **Keys**
phallus, and saw potent
sexual symbolism in it; but, in general,
visions of keys can be more variously
interpreted. To dream of one
symbolizes the unlocking of a problem,
or the solution to a difficulty.
Its message to the dreamer is that,
with patience, problems can always be
solved. For lovers, a key represents a
favorable sign – the "key" to their
partner's heart. However, to dream
of losing the key portends
storms in the romance and
the possible break-up of
the relationship.

King

Dreaming about a king symbolizes protection, and high masculine principles. It is common, therefore, to find that a king often represents your father, or a similar figure of authority from your childhood whom you admired. You may wish to seek guidance and help from them – their opinions should always be valued.

Kingfisher

The kingfisher is the legendary "halcyon" of mythology, whose presence in the land ensured a time of great happiness and plenty. Much of this ancient kudos still attaches itself to the bird, and to dream you see its plumage flash across the water signifies a change of fortune. Fate may have conspired against you, but your period of ill luck will soon end.

Kiss

This indicates a need for recognition. In most instances a kiss represents wish fulfilment, and you are expressing emotions that you would hesitate to show when awake. If the dream kiss is returned, it symbolizes happiness, and points to the emergence of a new romance (although not necessarily with the person you have kissed). To dream of kissing a partner you already love is considered a powerful omen of continued harmony.

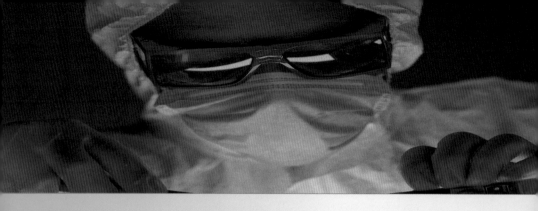

Laboratory

Mistrust of this subject stretches back to the days of Medieval alchemy – if you imagine yourself working in a laboratory in a dream, it is taken as an omen warning against putting too much time and effort into a doubtful project. The dream tells you to get out and live your life. Don't hold post-mortems; don't spend your time brooding over sorrows or mistakes; don't be the one who never gets things done!

Some dream analysts explain **ladder** the symbolism of a ladder as revealing a connection between the conscious and the unconscious mind; Sigmund Freud related climbing a ladder to sexual intercourse (moving up and down). It is most likely, however, that in your dream a ladder represents your aspiration to reach the highest rung of your chosen profession. To imagine descending the ladder implies you have aimed too high, too fast – try to pace yourself and you will eventually realize your goal. Falling from a ladder indicates a lack of self-belief in your own unique qualities.

Lake

If you dream about a lake, it is important to try to recall as much detail as possible on waking, as its appearance will decide if the symbol bodes for good or ill. A clear and tranquil lake points (as might be supposed) to good times and the fellowship of friends. However, a turbulent or murky lake denotes upheaval and problems.

To see a lake by moonlight augurs well for matters of the heart; but to wade out of your depth is a warning against promiscuity and over-indulgence. The lake has powerful mythical overtones – the "Lady of the Lake" delivered the sword Excalibur to King Arthur, and, at the end of his life, the sword was returned to her guardianship deep in its watery depths.

Language

To use excessively bad language, or swear constantly, in a dream (when you do not usually do so in waking life) implies extreme nervousness in the face of changing conditions. It can also denote difficulty in getting others to take you seriously.

Laughter

If you imagine yourself laughing in a dream, it symbolizes knowledge gained or a skill mastered. However, if people appear to be laughing at you, this may indicate low self-esteem, or simply be your mind's way of telling you to lighten up!

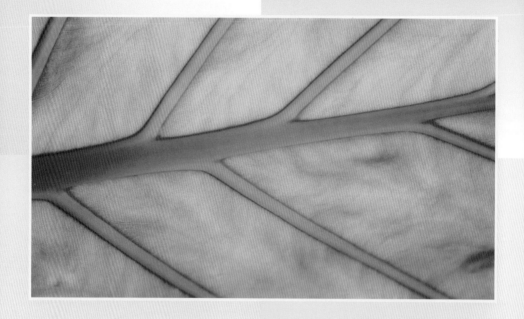

Leaf

Leaves are considered to be particularly reliable omens in dream lore. To see a fresh green leaf denotes good health – all nature smiles on you! Brown or withered leaves indicate changing fortune and separation from friends. Dreams of falling leaves are symbolic of a life being wasted, and this is interpreted as the mind encouraging the sleeper to act more positively.

Leaping

If you see yourself leaping over obstacles, it promises the achievement of your ambitions, but to jump and fall back shows that greater effort is required before you can attain your goal. To leap over the backs of people denotes arrogance and a willingness to use others for your own selfish ends.

Leeches

To dream that you have leeches attached to your body should be regarded as an inauspicious omen, symbolizing that someone is taking advantage of you and is, figuratively, "bleeding you dry." The more engorged on your blood the leech becomes, the greater will be the drain on you – from good to bad, from bad to worse!

Legs

Not unnaturally, to dream of shapely legs indicates desire – for women as well as for men. Injured legs are symbolic of poverty, while if you imagine you have thin legs, you are being warned about a forthcoming embarrassing situation.

Lemons

Jealousy and bitterness of the spirit are symbolized by dreams featuring lemons. They are generally an unfavourable omen, and to dream of them hanging from the tree could mean you are neglecting your health. To bite into the sour-tasting flesh foretells disappointments and humiliation; whereas to peel the fruit indicates the separation of lovers, or the caustic ending of a long friendship.

Lighthouse

A dream of a lighthouse shining against the blackness of the night, or as a beacon through thick fog, indicates that you will make wise decisions when confronted by choice. For those with problems, a vision of a lighthouse in a dream should be taken as a positive omen – indicating relief from their "storm-tossed" state, and safe guidance to calmer waters.

Both dream subjects have the common theme of a bright and guiding light, which directs the attention of the dreamer along a path the unconscious mind has chosen.

lightning

Native North Americans associate lightning with the universal spirit, the Thunderbird. In folklore, as in dreaming, the symbolism of lightning has long been associated with intuition and inspiration. To be struck by a thunderbolt in a dream implies the awakening realization that you possess psychic powers.

"*Once upon a time I, Chuang-tzu, dreamed I was a butterfly fluttering hither and thither, to all intent and purpose a butterfly. I was conscious only of following my fancies as a butterfly and was unaware of my individuality as a butterfly. Suddenly I was awakened and there I lay myself again. Now I do not know whether I was a man dreaming I was a butterfly or whether I am a butterfly now dreaming I am a man.*"

CHUANG-TSU   4TH-3RD CENTURY B.C.

The lion embodies the strength and valor of the animal kingdom; **Lion** it has featured in dream lore since Biblical times when it was regarded as a symbol of both royal authority and benevolent watchfulness. Nowadays, to dream of a lion is generally regarded as a favorable sign, indicating personal success or gain. However, this must be weighed against the possibility of antagonizing the beast – if angered, the benign nature of the omen is reversed with an implied risk of violent argument and mistrust.

Lips Dreaming of full, sensual lips indicates a person whose mood swings easily between extremes. Dreams of chapped, or cracked, lips indicate bitterness; licking your lips highlights greed and envy. For women, putting on lipstick has powerful sexual overtones – such a dream may be viewed as showing desire for a lustful encounter.

Love

In the realms of sleep, as in waking life, the need to love, and be loved, answers a universal longing. The first love we experience is parental love, and to dream of this symbolizes security and an upright character. Romantic love between partners represents loyalty and fidelity; a dream of loving your child indicates a return to innocence – with the promise of enduring joy. If love is seen to fail, it could be a subconscious warning of an argument that needs to be reconciled, lest the current rift becomes a yawning chasm.

A dream of being lucky is usually a highly **Luck** favorable omen, but it carries a note of warning that you should not leave too much to chance – the nature of luck is always to change! Various objects symbolize impending good fortune, and should be noted lest they occur in your dreams – picking up pins, horseshoes, flints and pebbles with holes through them, and four-leaf clovers, to name but a few. Take comfort if you dream of bad luck, as this usually portends a change which can only be for the better.

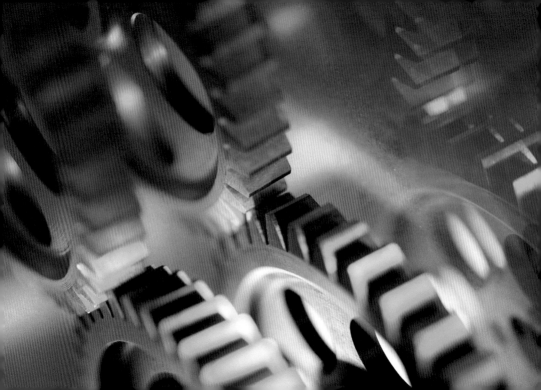

Machinery

Dreams involving machinery are usually considered to relate to the inner workings of the human body, with the more intricate areas relating to the brain. If the machine runs smoothly in your dream, all augurs well, but rusty, or broken, parts can be a warning to exercise or take better care of your health.

Madness

To imagine yourself to be mad in a dream should never be considered a malign prophetic omen – instead take comfort from the thought that it portends the exact opposite – analytical thought requires a sound mind. Usually a dream about madness reflects a humiliating experience in the past that filters through to the subconscious as unsettling images of lunacy.

Man

In sleep, the symbol of a man carries different meanings for male or female dreamer. In a man's dream he will represent an undefined aspect of the dreamer himself, perhaps possessing those qualities of "self" that the dreamer values, but more probably displaying faults – and holding them up for criticism. A woman dreaming of her idealized vision of a man reflects her "animus" – the male aspect of her psyche. In her early years, the animus is typically a physical athletic man, later "he" evolves into a romantic figure and, in middle age, is changed yet again into a spiritual, father-like figure.

"What a piece of work is a man! How noble in reason … in action how like an angel."
WILLIAM SHAKESPEARE, HAMLET, ACT II, SC II

Mansion

In the realms of sleep, the vision that you own a great house, or mansion, could indicate a conceited nature, and your subconscious is entreating you to be more realistic. Servants are synonymous with pomposity; and if one of the rooms in the mansion is felt to be haunted, this could point to a specific shortcoming in your personality.

Map

If you are of a fastidious disposition, you will find that your subconscious also appreciates an ordered approach. The symbolism of a map suggests that you are trying to find your way through life by charting its progress and striving to influence its direction. If the map appears confusing, this may reveal that in waking life you lack self-direction, and the path you have chosen seems to be heading nowhere. As a dream omen, it is claimed that the larger the map, the further the journey will be; similarly the more colorful the map is, the more rewarding the experience of travel will be.

Maps symbolize the desire to roam. The journey, however, may be one of self-discovery – representing fate and your future.

Marriage

If you are single, a dream of marriage is probably simple wishful thinking. As an omen for others, it is not the happy symbol that you might imagine, and indicates resentment and friction. Dream marriages often depict a union of opposites, reflecting both the masculine and feminine aspects of the dreamer's psyche, and if this aspect of "self" worries the dreamer, it is likely to manifest itself in the dark imagery of a forced wedding.

Mask

The mask is a symbol of the facade we choose to display to the world. Your true persona lies hidden beneath the mask and, as such, you must guard against feigned sincerity. It may also reveal a desire to let your own sexuality develop, but indicates that you fear the humiliation of rejection.

Meadow

Few places conjure up happier memories than a flower-filled meadow, and to dream of one indicates that you need to rejuvenate yourself by getting back in touch with nature. Meadow dreams encompass childhood memories that evoke the rapture we felt to be young and carefree. They reflect back to years of happiness, but also carry the warning to store up emotional provisions for less joyous times. Sunshine in a meadow foretells love that will be reciprocated.

"I know a bank whereon the wild thyme blows, where oxlips and the nodding violet grows ..." The flower meadows of Shakespeare's native countryside still abound with bloom – here one is dotted with the flowerheads of hawk weed and wild orchids.

Medicine

To dream that you are given medicine is interpreted as an optimistic omen, especially if it leaves a bitter taste in your mouth. The dream has that strange logic about it that argues that "anything that tastes bad must be doing some good!" The dream's symbolism implies that a person you once regarded as an obstacle will actually turn out to be a great asset. Paradoxically, to administer medicine in a dream portends causing pain to a close friend.

Mermaid

The mermaid symbolizes elusive feminine beauty. If a man dreams of one, she represents visions of the idealized woman – whom he feels he could love, but who he knows would reject him. She also stands for the "anima" – the feminine aspect of the male psyche. In a woman's dream, the mermaid is usually seen as a rival in love.

Message

In general, all dreams send messages from the unconscious using symbolism and prompts. However, to envision a direct written message is the most obvious "hint" the dreamer can receive. It is important to try to make sense of the message in the context of your own personal circumstances.

REMEMBER ME

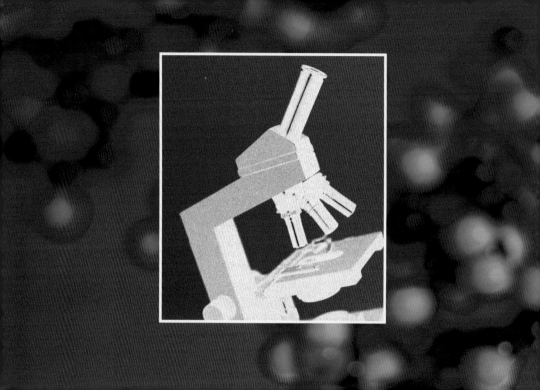

Microscope

Microscopes reveal a universe undreamed of by Blake or Dante. Their ability to scrutinize in minute detail serves to caution the dreamer – are they in danger of looking at things in too fine a detail, and over-looking the bigger picture? Or perhaps they read too much into one particular aspect of a situation and miss its wider perspective.

Milk

As a general symbol in dreams, milk represents comfort and support. However, at a subconscious level, it can be seen to represent a desire to be "mothered," and a nostalgic yearning for the emotional security and protection once enjoyed as a babe-in-arms. Alternatively, dreams of milk may (because of its color and consistency) have sexual connotations – representing masculine energy. In these instances, it symbolizes a desire for power and strength, rather than a need to be nurtured.

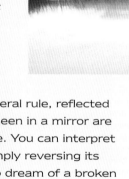

In this medieval woodcut (left) the Devil lies in wait to be reflected in the mirror's glass – a caution against the sin of vanity. Echoes of the mistrust once engendered by mirrors linger on in dreamscapes of the present day.

Mirror

As a general rule, reflected images seen in a mirror are to be considered false. You can interpret a mirror dream by simply reversing its apparent meaning. To dream of a broken mirror presages bad news and sadness.

Mist and Fog

A dream about being lost in dense mist or fog is surely one of the eeriest of visions. It is usually taken as a cry for help concerning a problem in waking life that is becoming obscured by irrelevances. Alternatively, your subconscious could be pointing out unseen dangers that you should identify, and so avoid stumbling over.

Moon

In most cultures throughout history the Moon has epitomized the mysterious aspect of the feminine – from Isis, the Great Mother of the Egyptians, to Christian iconography of the Virgin Mary. The Moon traditionally represents the emotional aspect of "self," and to dream of the "full-orbed moon in splendor" is considered a powerful symbol of peace and harmony. The open aspect of the full Moon echoes the circle, signifying wholeness and achievement in romance. A waxing Moon indicates female fertility and the desire for, or the possibility of, pregnancy – in the words of the ancients "the Moon is mother over all."

Samuel Palmer's mystical canvas "Cornfield by Moonlight with the Evening Star" illustrates the long-held belief that the waxing Moon radiates a magical glow that prompts crops to flourish and "the very earth to sing."

Money

In a dream, money signifies anything of value – health, energy, time, or self-esteem. Thus, being short of money symbolizes fear of failing health in old age, or lack of self-worth. Similarly, apprehension about splitting up a large bill for change could show an unwillingness to divide your energies – the note equates to your great potential, which is never actually spent (realized).

Monster

Monsters in your nightmares usually represent a darker aspect of your own psyche – perhaps a fear of death or the unknown – that is not confronted in waking life. If the monster is victimizing you in the dream, it may help to imagine returning to the dream, and to visualize fighting it. Killing the monster may eventually help resolve your phobia.

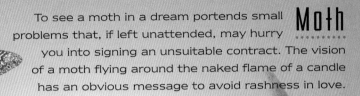

Moth

To see a moth in a dream portends small problems that, if left unattended, may hurry you into signing an unsuitable contract. The vision of a moth flying around the naked flame of a candle has an obvious message to avoid rashness in love.

Mountain

As in the real world, tall hills and mountains are viewed in dream lore as obstacles that must be surmounted. To dream you scale the "heights" to attain the summit signifies success in the work place and reaching the "peak" of your profession. However, to climb without gaining height is a message from the unconscious mind that you have set yourself unreasonable goals which you are unlikely to fulfil. To fall down a mountainside signifies that you have accepted the fact that old age is on its way.

Muscles

Muscles are symbols of strength for men, yet presage a life of hardship and toil when encountered in a woman's dream. For the male they imply struggle against enemies – in the workplace and in a sporting context – who will be overpowered. This adds to the confidence of the dreamer and may positively influence his waking life.

Mushrooms

To gather mushrooms foretells that small surprises awaiting the dreamer. In Western folklore they are associated with nature spirits, and to destroy one by accidentally treading on it is seen as a bad omen denoting misfortune and health worries.

Music

It is surprisingly common for people to dream about music, and it is invariably a positive sign. It indicates the level of harmony, or lack of it, that you currently experience in life. In many instances the dream is trying to tell us that we actually please our partners, although we may sometimes doubt it.

Nakedness

Dreaming that you are naked is one of the most common sleep experiences, and is usually interpreted as expressing either openness or vulnerability. By wanting to "reveal all," the subconscious may be trying to tell you to unburden yourself of something that has been bothering you. Maybe the dreamer has been unduly shy and reserved since childhood – perhaps as the result of a reprimand for some minor act of exhibitionism – and the dream is attempting to confront this anxiety and dismiss it as irrelevant. Another component of the dream may cause you to imagine yourself naked in a totally inappropriate setting. This reveals the dreamer's fear of embarrassment that others will gaze upon parts of their body that they feel to be inadequate.

Naturally, there is usually a sexual connotation in any dream where you imagine yourself to be naked. It could reflect a desire to remove your facade – to drop pretence and truly be yourself.

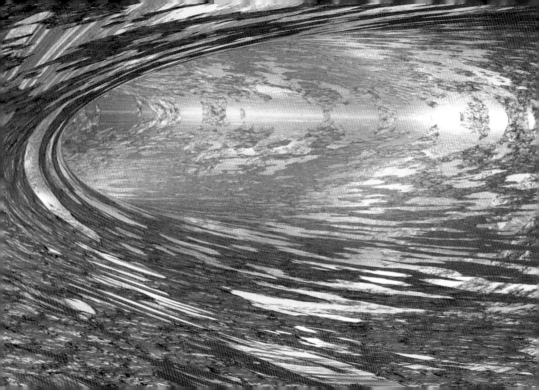

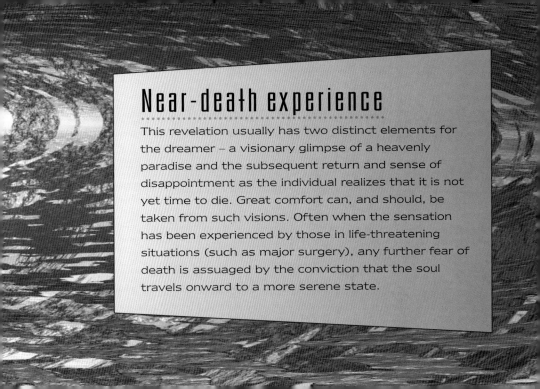

Near-death experience

This revelation usually has two distinct elements for
the dreamer – a visionary glimpse of a heavenly
paradise and the subsequent return and sense of
disappointment as the individual realizes that it is not
yet time to die. Great comfort can, and should, be
taken from such visions. Often when the sensation
has been experienced by those in life-threatening
situations (such as major surgery), any further fear of
death is assuaged by the conviction that the soul
travels onward to a more serene state.

Neck

The body and the head – respectively the domain of sexuality and of intellect – are connected by the neck. Consequently, quite naturally this area of the body is seen to symbolize a governing balance between impetuosity and restraint. The dreamer is perhaps seen to be "sticking their neck out" or "up to their neck in trouble;" either way the unconscious mind is trying to alert us to the problems into which desire, or lust, can unwittingly lead us. It is usually a warning not to take risks.

Nest

Nests offer a message regarding how dreamers see their homes. To view birds building a nest denotes a change of abode, whereas a destroyed nest shows latent aggression and a desire to break family ties. An empty nest, or one containing broken eggs, portends sorrow through the absence of friends.

The belief that in times of want the pelican fed its nestlings with its own blood to assuage their hunger makes the bird a poignant symbol of self-sacrifice. To the Medieval church the bird became emblematic of Christ.

Obedience

In earlier centuries, the quality of obedience was considered a virtue that ranked alongside those of valor, charity, and devotion to duty. In recent years however, the word "obedience" has assumed a more derogatory edge implying subservience, or lack of freedom. Thus, if you dream that you are obedient to another in a dream, it is seen as an ambiguous omen portending an uneventful period of time when your desires and wishes, although expressed, will be overlooked or ignored. This may induce dreams where you defer all decision-making to a dominant partner or parent, and thus feel excused, or absolved from, any subsequent choices that may go wrong.

Subconsciously you may wish to be "under-the-thumb" of another – as this passes responsibility to that person.

Orange

Oranges are thought to have been the golden apples of the Garden of the Hesperides in Greek mythology, and they have been associated with love and lust ever since. A dream of orange blossom may predict a wedding, and one of orange juice portends a short but passionate love-affair.

An orange tree laden with ripe fruit is seen a good omen, predicting a lasting relationship with a warm-hearted and imaginative partner.

For a dreamer to imagine eating an orange in a voracious manner forecasts a brief, lustful romance – short but sweet!

"*We are such stuff as dreams are made on*"

"In dreaming,
The clouds methought would open and show riches
Ready to drop upon me; that, when I wak'd
I cried to dream again...

...We are such stuff
As dreams are made on, and our little life
Is rounded with a sleep."

WILLIAM SHAKESPEARE 1564–1616

Orchard

Orchards are symbols of good fortune. To dream of one clothed in Springtime blossom presages the success of an ambition. If the orchard hangs heavy with ripened fruit, it points to the consolation that your years of toil and hard work will not pass unrewarded.

Orchestra

A dream of seeing yourself playing in an orchestra carries the obvious message that you need to keep in harmony with those around you – to comply with tradition at the expense of personal self-expression. If you lead the orchestra as conductor, this implies a desire to have others follow your commands.

Oyster / Pearl

In dreams, the relationship between the oyster and the pearl is viewed as a metaphor illustrating how beauty can be brought forth from ugliness. Their birth in the depths of the ocean implies hidden knowledge and esoteric wisdom; and the translucent nature and moon-like hue of the pearl allow them to stand for tears of joy or sorrow. Oysters are a noted dream-symbol of sexuality, and one source states that *"to imagine prizing open the oyster is a desire for seduction, regardless of consequence!"*

Pain

If you dream that you are in pain, your subconscious may be warning you not to take risks with your emotional or physical well-being. If you sense earache, it may herald the arrival of an unwelcome message, whereas pain in the eyes could indicate a family member who may need your support. Dreams where your body seems racked by pain or fatigue signify that you are worrying over trifling matters of little consequence while the best of life passes you by. They caution you not to invent troubles – imaginary ills are often harder to bear than actual ones.

Paralysis

This can be temporarily induced by an arm or leg "going to sleep" due to a trapped nerve. However, to dream of the sensation of being paralyzed seldom refers to a physical condition, but rather relates to the dreamer's subconscious. It may symbolize sexual inhibition – the greater the paralysis, the larger the concern abut impotence for men, or frigidity in women.

Parsley

As with dreams of most green things, parsley is an omen of advancement through hard work. To dream of eating it foretells enjoyable social gathering, while to pick parsley from a herb garden predicts an extravagant present.

Pea

Dreaming of peas indicates that an awkward decision will soon have to be made. This choice will become difficult because all options will appear to be of equal merit. Peas dried from seed are indicative of tenacity and strength of purpose; a dream of shelling peas indicates small joys that, despite their size and importance, invigorate the soul.

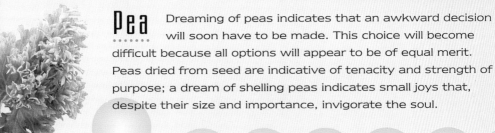

Peach

In the East, the peach is symbolic of a long and happy marriage. The Chinese god of long-life, Shou-hsing, is frequently depicted holding a peach plucked from the gardens of Paradise. Dream omens echo folk wisdom, so to imagine eating fresh peaches represents the probability of a lengthy and fulfilled marriage or partnership. However, if the fruit is seen to be bruised or sour, this is taken to signify vain hopes and a haunting acquaintance with melancholy.

Peacock

As a dream symbol, the peacock can be taken at face value; it represents a desire by the dreamer for more color and flamboyance in his or her waking life. It can, however, denote pride and vanity, and care should be taken lest these characteristics overtake you. A peacock may also imply that the dreamer is currently aware of an attractive admirer.

Pepper

Red peppers in a dream indicate human warmth and sociability, whereas green peppers intimate that sensible precautions should be taken. To burn your tongue with pepper or chilli is interpreted as a warning to temper harsh words with moderate actions.

Piano

To dream of playing the piano and enjoying its music augurs well for the future, and can signify the discovery of something of value hidden in an unlikely place. To play badly, or out of tune, indicates an anxiety that you lack the skills necessary to succeed in your chosen field.

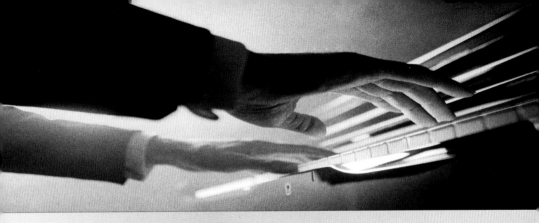

Despite the slur that pigs are dirty,
lazy creatures with gluttonous
appetites, to dream of them has long been
held to be a positive omen, denoting good
health and successful ventures. To see a full
litter of piglets represents joyfulness.

Pig

Pilgrimage

To go on pilgrimage is as much a journey of self-discovery for the dreamer, as it is an expression of religious duty. The Medieval goal of achieving remission of sins by traveling to revere the bones of a saint or martyr is mirrored by the sleeper who attempts to use the symbolism of pilgrimage and expiation to exorcize the psyche of past "sins" and misdemeanors.

As in dreams, the Medieval stained glass of England's Canterbury Cathedral floods the eye with graphic imagery – explaining by means of symbols the complex issues and morality of the age to those unable to understand the written word.

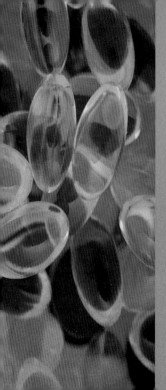

Pills

Pills in a dream are often thought to symbolize a forthcoming venture. The pills' use (for medical purposes) or abuse determine the omens – and thus the success of the enterprise. To dream of a bottle of pills that you cannot open reflects indecision and a timid nature – you are the only person who doubts your abilities, so a little more confidence in your own qualities would go a very long way.

Planet

If you dream of visiting a strange planet, it could indicate that you may soon be exposed to exciting new opportunities. The dream indicates that your ambitions, goals, and aims in life are all attainable; a subsequent move of house, or job, would seem to be indicated.

Poison

Predictably, poison is seldom a good omen, and if in your dreams you sense that you have been poisoned, this may be taken as a sign that others scheme against you. Alternatively, if it is you who murders by poison – a rival in love perhaps – then you and your lover will soon be parted by jealousy. The crime also presages trouble from an unexpected source. Rather surprisingly however, imagining that you see others poisoned indicates a release from your present worries.

Politician

For some, dreaming of becoming a politician could be classed a "nightmare;" while, for others, life in the public eye would be welcomed – and to achieve the highest office, a dream come true! Thus, the portent depends upon how you rate the politician's value to society. In general, the omens are not good, and foretell duplicity and the enmity of friends. If you dream of political debates, be cautioned – for you risk ruin by falsehood and ingenious flattery.

In Roman mythology the poppy is associated with Morpheus, the god of dreams; it was once thought that staring into the vivid red bloom would induce sleep. In dream lore the flower is viewed with suspicion (doubtless a reflection upon those members of the plant's family which are narcotic), and it is interpreted as an omen of temptation and short-lived happiness. Plucked flowers soon shed their petals —so to receive a gift of poppies signifies a brief and unfulfilling encounter.

Poppy

Potatoes

It is unsurprising to learn that potatoes – one of the staple foods of life – have come to represent stability in the home, and earthy responses to earthy problems. A dream of harvesting a potato crop indicates success through toil, to plant them in the soil denotes prudence but if the crop is rotten the future is seen to be bleak.

Profits

Hopes of making fabulous profits from astute investments fill many nighttime dreams, just as they do our daydream fantasies. The lure of easy money is a universal theme, but one about which our dreams seek to warn us. Just as there are no "free lunches" in life so we should remember to be on our guard against expecting "something for nothing," and letting greed rule our actions.

Quarrel

To engage in an argument or quarrel in a dream is usually unsettling. Any unpleasantness, however, must not be taken at face value, but should rather be viewed as a release of pressures built up in our waking life. In dreams those worries that we refuse to acknowledge are brought to the fore and given violent release. If you argue, beware of losing your temper as this may lead to decisions you will live to regret.

Quarry and Mining

The need to hew materials from the earth has existed since our prehistoric ancestors first looked to flint for tool making. In dream lore the nature of the material that is being mined or quarried determines the dream's significance. Chalk presages possible financial losses, while to see a stone quarry suggests you should anticipate a long journey.

A coal mine in a dream denotes that your present low spirits will soon be lifted, and fortune will shine upon you. However, to mine gold or silver foretells goals that remain tantalizingly out of reach.

Queen

The unconscious mind may use the symbol of a regal and powerful woman (possibly even a mother figure) to highlight the dreamer's need to be recognized as an individual. Dreams in which a monarch, or a person of similar prestige, visits your home are commonly experienced, and imply that the sleeper feels overlooked and would appreciate more attention.

Rabbits

In dreams a rabbit is usually a harbinger of good luck, and its renowned ability to reproduce symbolizes prosperity and fertility. Rabbits, however, can also send a warning to dreamers that their fears can actually bring about the circumstance of which they are frightened.

Race

A race indicates that the dreamer is aware of a rival who seeks the same objectives as themselves. As a dream omen it is important to strive to defeat other competitors – only in this way will you be assured of success.

If you show true competitive spirit and a will to win, positive thoughts from your dreamscape will spill over into the waking world.

Each dreamer reacts to the emotion of rage in a different way – from simmering disquiet to the full, red-faced anger that makes you want to pull your hair out. It is rarely a fortunate omen to envision, and unless a degree of restraint moderates the dreamer's rage, it portends unhappiness and discord, with implicit warnings about the dangers of losing self-control. Since hatred and rage poison the soul, don't nourish enmities or bear grudges. In life try to avoid people and circumstances that you know will make you unhappy.

Rage

Rain and Rainbows

Although its legendary "crock of gold" may prove elusive, to dream of rainbows, or rain, is considered a particularly lucky omen. Rain in a dreamscape portends "blessings descending" and it is often regarded as the "tears of the spirit" which flow to wash away fears and worries.

The celestial appearance of the rainbow was seen by our ancestors as proof of a benign deity. Because it spanned heaven and earth, it became a potent symbol, which in dream lore has come to be regarded as an exceedingly fortuitous omen. To dream of its seven colors denotes healing.

Raspberry

Dreams of picking raspberries warn the sleeper to make the most of life's small pleasures; to imagine eating the fruit foretells an entanglement that will prove difficult, if not impossible, to unravel.

"But there's a tree of many, one,
A single field which I have looked upon,
Both of them speak of something that is gone:
The pansy at my feet
Doth the same tale repeat:
Whither is fled the visionary gleam?
Where is it now, the glory and the dream?

Our birth is but a sleep and a forgetting;
The Soul that rises with us, our life's Star,
Hath had elsewhere its setting."

WILLIAM WORDSWORTH 1770–1850

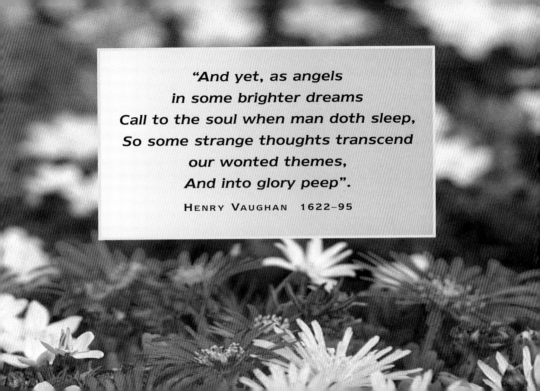

"And yet, as angels
in some brighter dreams
Call to the soul when man doth sleep,
So some strange thoughts transcend
our wonted themes,
And into glory peep".

HENRY VAUGHAN 1622–95

Reflections

To see a reflection of something or someone in the calm waters of a lake or river must be taken as a warning about the transient nature of the object, or the fickle character of the individual. The merest breeze can ruffle the waters, and the image is lost for ever. The vision cautions against putting faith in unworthy friends.

A dream in which you are # Rescue
rescued from a dangerous
situation usually indicates that you feel
indebted to someone. Often the rescuer
is a person whom we particularly admire
(perhaps someone famous or in the
public eye) whose selfless act on our
behalf serves to bolster the high esteem
in which we hold them. If you dream that
you are rescuing someone, this reflects a
desire for a closer relationship or sexual
contact with that person – a wish
fulfilment dream that is echoed in
romantic literature by the inordinate
swarms of damsels in distress who fall
in love with their heroic rescuer.

To dream of exacting # Revenge

revenge upon a personal rival is regarded as characteristic of a weak and uncharitable disposition, one that the dreamer should make every effort to remedy. A lust for revenge can also reveal an obsessive nature which, if not kept carefully in check, may cause you to make powerful enemies and lose the regard of those who love and admire you.

In dreams, revenge may consist of an ingenious reprisal that you feel pays back the victim. It is, however, an empty victory that bodes well for neither party.

River

A river seen in a dream may be interpreted as a metaphor for life. Clear, untroubled waters indicate purity and strength, but blackish water points to the fact that someone is exercising a baleful influence over the dreamer. Straight and swift-flowing rivers signify honest toil, whereas a sluggish flow, that twists and turns, is viewed as an inauspicious omen indicating pleasure found in unusual places.

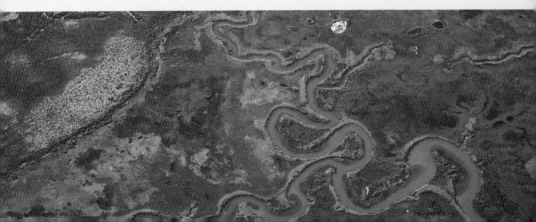

Road

The vision of an open road stretching out in front of the dreamer symbolizes the individual "way," or destiny that leads to the realization of personal aims in life. A smooth, straight road indicates a life of harmony; whereas a rough or winding road may appear more interesting, but be fraught with countless trials and tribulations.

Other details along the route offer insight into the direction in which the dreamer's life is heading. Forks and turnings could force you from the beaten track, and dead-ends lead you nowhere. Rocks and other obstacles might halt your progress. The road may be an uphill struggle of constant exertion, or a downhill stroll with the implicit danger of the dreamer being pulled dangerously out-of-control.

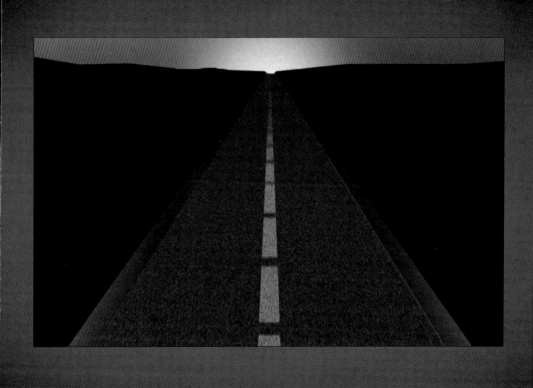

Rocks

A classic obstacle dream in which the rocks stand for danger or difficult times ahead that must be surmounted. The unconscious appeals to dreamer not to let themself be defeated by what might appear to be insurmountable problems. Alternatively, the rocks can represent the emotional sterility of the dreamer's life which, after a long period of harmony, has become so limiting that it feels as though they they have reached a dead end.

Rose

Roses are tokens of love, and to receive a gift of them in a dream is symbolic of being loved both physically and spiritually. In dream lore roses also denote female sexuality and virginity (the rosebud). To see into the heart of a red rose may be a dream echo of our earliest prenatal memory – enclosed within the satin folds of the womb.

Rowing

To imagine yourself rowing in a dream indicates that you have made a determined effort to complete a project that is important to you. Furthermore, to row steadily and easily indicates that you are very much aware of your abilities and talents, and are prepared to exploit them to the full.

Running

For a jogger, or casual runner,
to dream about their sport may
be the ultimate running "high."
You can become as light as a
feather – as though you have
wings on your feet. Such feelings
presage a burning ambition that is
yet to be achieved. Alternatively,
you may experience feet-of-lead –
your slow progress represents a very
common anxiety dream, where an
attempt to run away from something
unpleasant leaves you apparently
rooted to the spot.

Sadness

Many emotions are experienced as intensely in dreams as they are in waking life. However, most authorities concur that if a dreamer feels sadness, it is a classic paradoxical dream, which turns the dreamer's "long-face" on its head and promises the bright prospect of a period of fun and enjoyment.

Like angels, a saint may appear in your dream as a guardian spirit that looks over # Saint

you. Their role as personal protectors may offer consolation to the dreamer, but they also act as a warning to return to conventional values. Morally they imply the threat of censure. You should live well, and honestly – in short, to follow their saintly example in thought and in deed.

Sand

This may symbolize indecision or the passage of time, and reflect the many small trials and tribulations which arise because you can never find enough hours to fit into the day. To feel wet sand against your body, or in your clothing, is a warning against being exploited by a friend; while to dream that you walk along an expanse of sand suggests a suspicious mind prone to jealousy.

Scales represent # Scales
equilibrium between the
spiritual and the physical. The vision of a
pair of scales in a dream usually has a
literal meaning, and symbolizes a need to
weigh up all considerations before
arriving at a considered judgment.
Alternatively, the dream may represent
justice which you feel is being denied to
you in your waking life.

The imagery of scales has been used since
Egyptian times. Anubis, guardian of the dead,
weighed the worth of a man's heart (his soul)
against a feather – those that passed the test
were granted safe passage to the afterlife…
those that failed were damned!

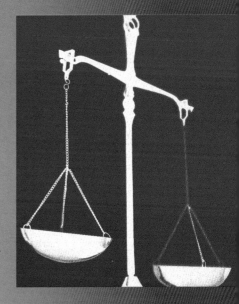

Scent and Perfume

The least-used and appreciated of our senses, nothing has the power to evoke memory better than smell. Dream images become intensified if enhanced by scent – whether the fragrance of a wild flower, the perfume of a loved one, or the memory of grandfather's pipe tobacco. It is invariably the unconscious mind's attempt to remind the dreamer of a distant but important memory. Try to learn from the emotional response evoked.

Scissors

In male adolescence, to dream of scissors may reflect a deep-seated concern about growing toward manhood. Fears of castration by sharp objects are not uncommon at this age, but the dream imagery more usually refers to feelings of being "cut off" from past childhood. For other dreamers, scissors can be taken as a warning not to divide your attention between two ambitions, or you will achieve neither.

Scorpion

Small unforeseen vexations may have enormous repercussions out of all proportion to their size. To see a scorpion is a warning that those problems you wish to keep hidden will not simply

vanish because they are no longer visible. The creature can also denote tremendous tenacity in pursuing an objective.

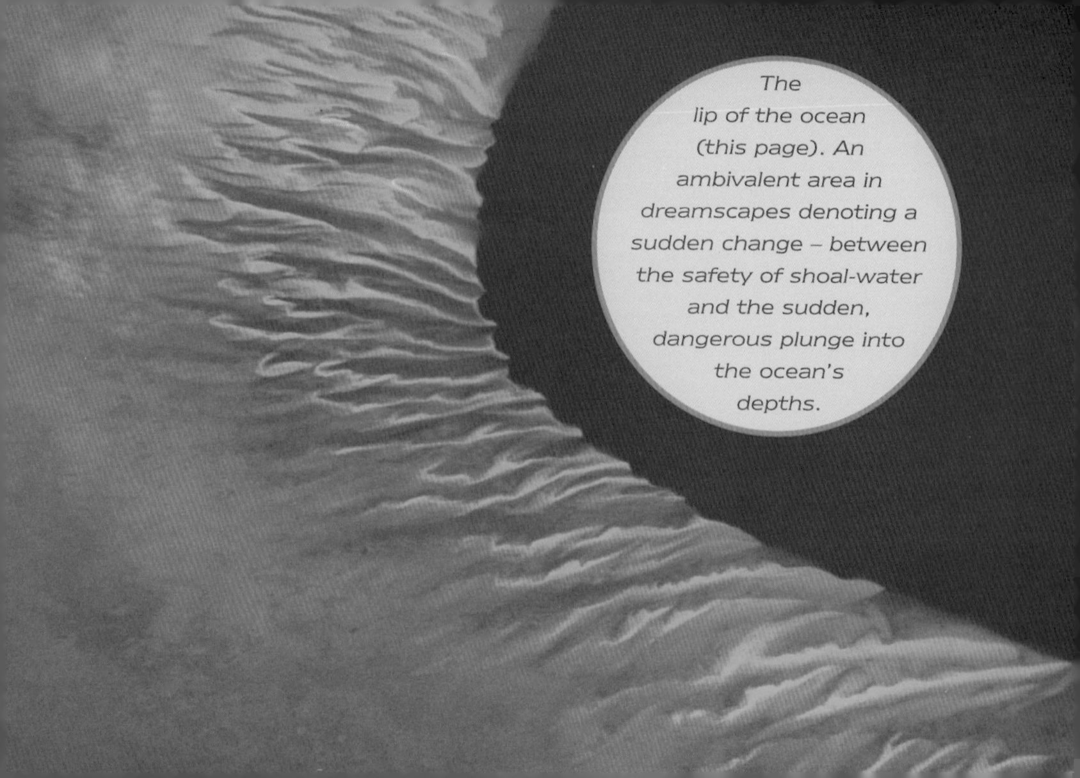

The
lip of the ocean
(this page). An
ambivalent area in
dreamscapes denoting a
sudden change – between
the safety of shoal-water
and the sudden,
dangerous plunge into
the ocean's
depths.

Sea / Ocean

These symbolize emotions, and the mystical power of the psyche. Most authorities agree that in dreams of the sea or the ocean, it is the state and depth of the water that are critical to interpreting the omens. The water's depth distinguishes between the profound and the superficial (shallow). Similarly, to dream of a calm surface is a favorable portent for an enterprise or relationship, whereas stormy waters offer far less encouragement.

Dream lore associates seeds with growth and prosperity – no matter how bad

Seed

conditions might be. They symbolize the germ of an idea that, if nurtured, will provide a golden opportunity for advancement. Such opportunities occur rarely, and should be seized – they represent the chance of a better and more fulfilling life.

Sex

Freud saw sexual symbolism in virtually every dream topic; from the masculinity of rearing serpents or keys in a lock, to the feminine charms of dark boxes or silk purses (and, perhaps, sow's ears!).

Taking a wider view, most experts now consider dreams of sexual activity to mainly express wish fulfilment. However, this is not to devalue them as they can serve as emotional safety valves, or act as an implied reproach against practices, partners, or perversions your subconscious finds unacceptable.

Dreaming of deformed genitals is thought to warn against over-indulgence; while to imagine exposing your sexual organs is regarded as a caution to guard against indiscretion.

Shaking hands

To shake hands in a dream is not necessarily the comforting image the dreamer might imagine it to be. The action cautions the sleeper to question the motives of those around him – good manners often mask a hard heart.

Shark

Film and popular literature have conspired to blacken the image of this formidable predator. Crimson blood-flow and violent thrashing in foam-covered water are perceived as the inevitable outcome of their unseen pursuit. It may be an exaggerated fear (more people are killed by elephants each year than by sharks) but our subconscious thrives upon the Gothic. Thus, to dream of a shark denotes enemies that seek to ambush you; to be attacked by one portends reverses that will sink all hope and ambition.

Ships

The ship in your dreams represent "self" – the dreamer as a whole. Thus, the nature of any voyage reflects the circumstances of the dreamer's current life. "Going off to sea" may symbolize a search for freedom and independence; whereas storms and turbulent seas that keep your ship in port can indicate a reluctance to leave the family home. In dreams, cargo ships are laden with temptation, cruise liners augur family resentments, and a battleship portends the death of a romance.

To dream of a shipwreck may be your subconscious' way of graphically bringing to an end one phase of your life, in readiness for the next.

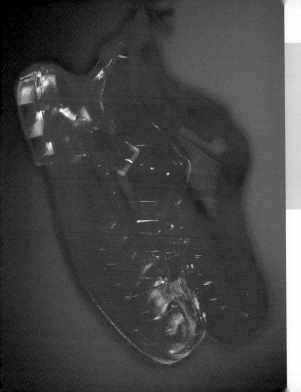

Shoes

Shoes are an integral part of the steps we take along life's path, and dreams of them are seen as indicators of what the future holds. Tight shoes, for example, may indicate problems with money, while a dream of children's shoes can foretell a change of address. Shabby or soiled footwear augurs a clash of personalities, and a loose pair indicates that the dreamer is wasting time and money on an ill-conceived enterprise.

Skating

This dream is generally considered a premonition of troubled times ahead. If you see yourself skating on ice, be wary as it may indicate that a relationship is about to be threatened by someone who is envious of your success. Alternatively, to see others skating foretells that people you thought were friends will spread gossip about you. If the ice cracks, or is seen to break, act cautiously upon advice offered in confidence.

"All things to end are made ..."
– images that once had the power
to terrify the Medieval mind, in our
darkest dreams terrify still!"

Skeleton

It would be unusual if our preoccupation with death were not to enter the realms of sleep. To dream of a skeleton is the mind's way of reminding ourselves of our own mortality and the fleeting vanity of the moment – *"beauty is a flower, which worms will devour."*

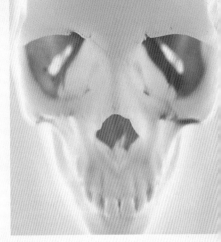

Skin

Evocative of touch and sensual pleasure, the skin is one of the symbols chosen by the unconscious mind to inform dreamers that they need to come to terms with their own sexuality. It shows an underlying awareness of their bodies, and the need to shed some inhibitions. Perhaps you are in danger of being regarded as insular and puritanical when you would benefit from more open displays of warmth and emotion.

Skull

A skull – the shell of death – appears in dreams to remind us that if we agonize over small details, we may lose sight of the broader picture. Things must no be taken at face value – appearances can be deceptive – beware of forming shallow opinions.

Sky

The interpretation of a dream featuring the sky depends upon its appearance – the old adage about "storm clouds gathering" portends an unsettling period of hardship for the dreamer; blue sky (the clearer the better) offers the prospect of a brief but happy respite from life's problems. Simply to stare into its blue vastness signifies avoidance of responsibility, or indicates a latent creative force within you that needs stimulation.

Sleep

To dream of being asleep may indicate that some part of the dreamer's personality lies hidden, or has died (is dormant). Perhaps your subconscious is telling you to awaken that which has been locked away – to renew your faith, or regain the sense of fun that over the years persistent worries might have dulled.

Perhaps no other symbol has so many varied and diverse interpretations. The snake is a contradiction – its bite can be deadly, yet when twined around a staff it symbolizes healing. Serpents represent wisdom but are condemned for their role in the Biblical Fall of Man. In dark dreams they reflect fears of impotence and sexual anxiety; or highlight the sleeper's phobia still further by the magnification of their supposed malign powers. If you remain unafraid you will become "knowledgeable without being knowing."

Snake

Snow

To dream of snow signifies purity and innocence, but slush or dirty snow implies guilt and a remorseful mind. To see the landscape covered in snow denotes a fresh beginning, but one that must be acted upon quickly or the chance will fade away.

Soldier

A dream about soldiers could indicate inner conflict; you may desire greater discipline and structure within your life. Alternatively, the symbolism may be seen to offer a legitimate outlet for aggression, with the incentive of comradeship and the possibility of heroism. To dream you are wounded is a positive omen, denoting both initiation and acceptance by your peers.

Son

As with the symbol of a daughter, a son represents the dreamer's "inner child." The boy represents the masculine side of the dreamer's persona, and the aspirations of the parent (the dreamer) will be reflected in the son's achievements. Likewise, any failures or dangers faced by the child will also have repercussions for the dreamer.

Song

To hear a song in a dream signifies consolation in adversity, and the recovery of the dreamer to full health if he or she is unwell. Should the song be mournful, or out of tune, it points to possible problems and worries that lie in wait just around the corner – fortunately these are unlikely to trouble you for very long, and will soon be resolved.

The rapturous plain-song of angels (left), or the sad dirge of wind-blown trees – in dreams, song encompasses a wide spectrum of sounds, each of which evokes its own particular resonance.

Space

To envision traveling through the boundless infinity of space is at once exhilarating and unnerving. It is usually understood to predict a long and severe struggle ahead for the dreamer, but one that will free them from a confining situation and bring eventual release. Thus, as an omen, space offers the promise of independence and new-found freedom.

*"The Magic
Appte Tree,"
by Samuel Palmer
circa 1830*

*"We are like the chrysalis asleep,
and dreaming of its wings"*

*"There was a time when meadow, grove, and stream,
The earth, and every common sight,
To me did seem
Apparelled in celestial light,
The glory and the freshness of a dream."*

Space Shuttle

Dreams of adventurous expeditions
are a straightforward sign of the
dreamer's desire for challenging
new horizons. It is interesting to
note how the subconscious adapts
to keep pace with innovation. In the
19th century the symbol that
appeared was invariably a ship;
50 years ago it was an aircraft; but
today dreamers often report that
the cutting-edge technology of the
Space Shuttle is the subconscious
symbol that represents their thirst
for excitement and adventure.

Spider

Love them or loathe them, a spider in your dreams (or nightmares) represents the qualities of patience and tenacity. Surprisingly, however, to dream of harming a spider is considered an omen of imminent good news – which turns on its head the superstition that killing a spider brings bad luck. Perhaps even more bizarre is the belief held in some quarters that actually to eat a spider is indicative of a voluptuous personality.

Sport

Dreams involving sporting activity should never be taken at face value, as they do not always relate to athletic prowess. Research has established that sporting success can be used as a metaphor for achievements at work, or in the home. It reveals your competitive edge and shows how you play the game of life. To dream of participating in team sports shows emotional commitment, and if you see yourself winning, this should be viewed as a favorable omen that may have an influence on your waking life.

Spots

Our appearance is the first thing other people notice about us. Spots and blemishes are often blown up out of all proportion to the actual significance of such minor irritants. Our unconscious reflects this unease, and so to see spots in a dream denotes trifling worry over nothing.

Spring is the season of renewed energy and regrowth, traditionally associated with childhood and early youth. A dream of Spring is an auspicious omen that implies the desire to start afresh, perhaps with renewed optimism in a new job; or in affairs of the heart where a new, lighter touch will lead to refreshed commitment. After a dream in which Spring appears, it is worth pursuing the new project that you have had at the back of your mind for ages but were reluctant to start, now is a good time to act – fortune will look kindly upon any enterprise you undertake.

Spring

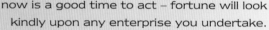

Stab

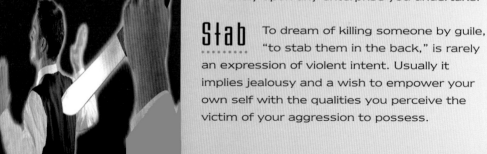

To dream of killing someone by guile, "to stab them in the back," is rarely an expression of violent intent. Usually it implies jealousy and a wish to empower your own self with the qualities you perceive the victim of your aggression to possess.

Stairs

The implications of "going up in the world," or "heading for a fall," are clearly implicit in dreams relating to stairs. Climbing them foretells a rise in rank or authority; a descent probably implies a loss of recognition and confidence. If you dream that you slip and fall on stairs, it may indicate that you have become emotionally involved in another's problem and need to be more detached.

Spiral stairs combine the positive symbolism of ascendancy (rising) with that of eternity (the circle).

Stars

Stars have been thought to guide Man's destiny since earliest times. In dreams their appearance portends a birth (either physical or symbolic), or represents a striving to achieve some important personal goals – hence "wishing on" or "striving for" a star. To see a five-pointed star in your dreams could denote magical guidance, and a six-pointed star (the traditional Star of David) may indicate that the physical and the spiritual sides of your psyche will shortly be brought into greater balance.

Storm

As in life, storms in dreams are ill omens that hint at outbursts of emotions, anger, or danger at the hands of raging natural forces. An approaching storm, whether it be of hail or snow, rain or wind, is a sure sign that trouble awaits, and you should remain extra-cautious for the next few days. If the storm is seen to pass, or blows itself out, then your affliction will be less severe.

A dream of strawberries, or of giving them to someone, is a favorable sign indicating that a pleasant surprise will come your way. To eat the fruit denotes requited love for a man, and for a woman presages pregnancy and the delivery of a son.

Strawberry

Summer

Dreaming of Summer is indicative of spiritual insight, and the warmth of emotional fulfilment. It is not just in mythology that the "Summer Land" is seen as a place of profound goodness – it is a landscape reflected in our dreams also, where every vista offers the reward of a bounteous harvest.

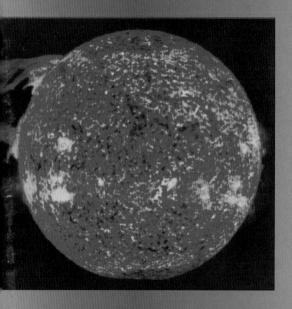

Sun

It is the giver of light, energy, and life; to dream of the Sun is always an encouraging omen, meriting special attention. It could represent the glory of God, or the light of the intellect – either should be viewed as the opening of a door to new opportunities and challenges in life – a promise of exciting changes that foretell success. To view the Sun obscured by cloud, however, indicates unexpected obstacles placed in your path that could lead to your downfall.

In Western mythology the swan symbolizes the White Goddess, who stands for poetry and song. The bird's whiteness represents purity and sincerity.

Swan

A dream of these magnificent snow-white birds has been considered a fortunate omen for centuries. In dream lore they have become a symbol of transformation – indicating the psyche's progression to higher levels of consciousness. Thus, the swan is seen as an encouragement to dreamers to allow their spiritual progression to occur naturally – to let intuition gently guide them. However, a vision of an injured swan in a dream is taken as a warning against complacency and self-satisfaction.

Sweetheart

The term "sweetheart" may seem strangely old-fashioned, but it perfectly describes that time of innocence and love when the first faltering steps on the road to adult relationships were taken.

To dream of a sweetheart represents maturity and confidence – of feeling at ease with your emotions. Indeed, such may be the memory of the first flutterings of love, that its image returns intermittently to haunt your dreams into old age – a yardstick by which other encounters are measured.

Swimming

Swimming is probably as near as most people come to experiencing what it must feel like for a bird to fly. Thus, in sleep, it takes on much of the symbolism associated with dreams of flight. Swimming can be a sensual activity (Freud equated it with sexual intercourse), and to feel relaxed and comfortable in the water bodes well for a happy relationship. However, if you feel "out of your depth," this indicates that you and your partner are probably not compatible.

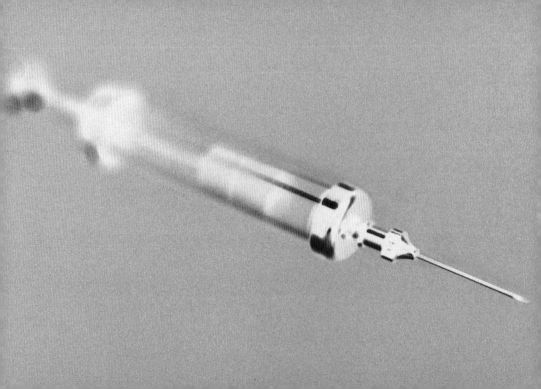

Sword

The weapon is symbolic of the dreamer's defense against problems, and the ability to cope in difficult situations. The more strongly the sword is brandished, the more the dreamer is seen to resort to the intellect rather than raw emotion.

Syringe

Fear of needles, and a sense of "bodily invasion," make a dream about injections an awkward one to interpret. Despite exaggerated perceptions of pain, a syringe is medically used for our benefit, and thus it is often taken to signify that worries about health matters are not such a problem as we may originally have feared. It serves also to underline the message that, in life, small trials and tribulations are to be endured for the greater good.

Talking to famous people

If you dream that you are in conversation with famous people, either living or from the past, it indicates an anxiety that others do not take you seriously. By associating with those you hold in high regard, you are elevated from obscurity to importance, basking in their reflected glory – you are the one with whom "they" have chosen to spend time!

Teeth

Simple anxiety about a forthcoming dental appointment may cause us to dream of teeth. If this is not the case, a dream of losing a tooth, or of them all falling out, may indicate fears of losing something important – the dreamer's health, looks, or potency. In essence, teeth (or lack of them) highlight concern about aging.

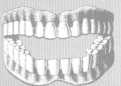

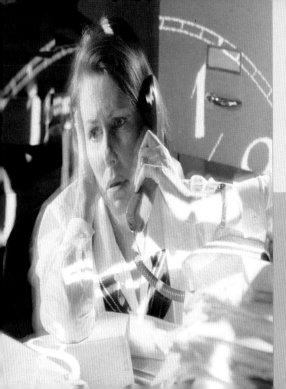

Telephone

The appearance of a telephone in a dream may indicate that you are anxious to make contact with someone, but hesitate to do so lest they reject your advances. Alternatively, it may highlight the stress telephones can cause in our waking lives as they relay a constant flow of problems that demand to be sorted out. To imagine you hear garbled, or indistinct, messages is a dream omen that portends small differences of opinion that might lead to a much larger rift.

Tiger

William Blake's dread beast of *"fearful symmetry"* – the tygre – has symbolized ferocity and animal energy throughout history, as well as vitality and protectiveness. In dreams its interpretation depends upon the tiger's demeanor – if it is benign or tamed, it signifies that a person in authority will aid your social advancement, but if the beast is stalking or attacking, this is usually taken as a sign of hidden dangers lurking on the horizon. However menacing or terrifying the dream may be, there is always the encouragement to those facing even the fiercest adversity that they can, with determination, succeed.

Time

In the realms of our dreams "time" and "chronological sequence" seldom present themselves as we order them in our waking lives. The dreamer's path is a serendipitous walk, where past, present, and future may be telescoped into a single dream. A greater understanding of how your dreams use time is always a useful aid to prediction.

Tomatoes

Tomatoes are dream omens of comfort and ease. The ripe fruit indicates encouragement, while fresh ones denote a healthy mind in a healthy body. Picking tomatoes in a dream symbolizes relaxed optimism, and to eat them augurs well for a successful venture.

Treasure

Treasure is often an omen that the dreamer will succeed after strenuous effort. The treasure, however, is unlikely to be wealth, but will represent whatever is most worthwhile to the dreamer, love or spiritual values – perhaps even life itself!

Trees "root" us into a unique relationship with the land, and offer **Tree**
insight into the mysteries of the natural world. Trees are one of
the most common dream symbols, and a tree seen in full-leaf majesty
signifies prosperity. In folklore they often take on human qualities and have
come to represent humanity's highest aspirations (branches reaching

skywards) or basest, earthly
desires (the soiled tangle of
roots). To imagine planting
trees foretells a new romance;
young saplings are a good
omen, especially in relation to
the possibility of moving house.
If a sleeper dreams that a
single leaf floats down and
rests upon them, this is a lucky
omen in matters of the heart.

This loud and brassy instrument # Trumpet
delivers an appropriate message
for the dreamer – to beware of "blowing your own
trumpet" in case, by your boastful and conceited
actions, you alienate those people around you
whose friendship and loyalty you can least afford
to lose. Be yourself, not an "image" of yourself!

Umbrella
Symbolic of shelter and
security, the umbrella
appears in our dreams to reveal the need for
the dreamer to listen to the advice of well-
meaning friends. Heeding their opinions will help you to face up to
responsibility. Umbrellas further warn that the dreamer should be watchful
of taking themselves too seriously – don't think that for some reason you
should be protected from the misfortunes that befall others.

Your subconscious may tell you to take shelter, not only against the elements but also from the pain of scorn and ridicule.

Underwater

Three decades ago, hardly any dreams featuring the underwater world were recorded. However, the growing interest in sea-life television programs, and the increased popularity of diving, have brought the subject to the public eye. As a topic it says much about the psyche of the dreamer, and is rich in symbolism.

The undersea world is so unlike our own that to dream of being there is to escape the tedium of everyday life, and experience a world of constantly changing color and form. To float weightless (almost like an embryo) in this new environment indicates a desire to retreat – to be beguiled into forgetting the troubled, storm-tossed waters overhead.

Undressing

This is one of the most common elements of the dreamscape, and a theme which plays upon the dreamer's insecurities about their body, and the fear that exposure of personal secrets will bring public ridicule. The dreamer may feel an overwhelming need to cover up but, as is the nature of such things, the harder they try to regain some semblance of respectability, the more exposed they actually become.

Unicorn

By its nature this mystical beast represents the lunar and feminine, yet its rampant horn is seen as signifying male supremacy over the female. Thus, in dreams, it denotes conflict that will remain unresolved.

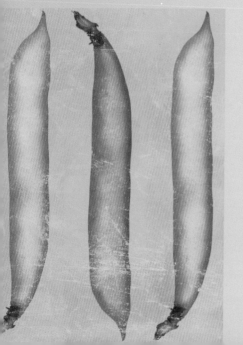

Vegetables

Dreams of such "down to earth" plants seldom bodes well. Dreamers may think that they have been resourceful and prudent, but given time to reflect fully, they will come to realize that they have been duped and imposed upon.

Village

This is a very propitious dream subject, and promises harmony, creation of good family foundations, and the confident expectation of a dignified old age. To imagine that you live within your dream village foretells pleasant fellowship and reunion with old friends.

Vine

A dream of a vineyard full of ripe grapes is an omen of prosperity and living life to the full. To pick and eat the grapes, however, presages hardship and folly. Folklore states the first grape harvest was gathered by a lion, a lamb, and a hog – henceforth man received from wine the characteristics of ferocity, mildness and wallowing in the mire!

Violin

To dream that you hear a violin serenade indicates a longing for romance in your life. Playing the instrument yourself is taken as a message that you need to try to gain the independence that you currently lack, and which will prove vital to your future aspirations.

Virgin

Often the symbol of the virgin is depicted in dream lore playing a lyre or a flute, and, because she is often confused with the Virgin Mary, frequently wearing a crown of stars. The virgin also represents the *"genius loci"* (the protecting deity) of some holy place. To win her trust augurs well for the dreamer, and to embrace her is considered a talisman of good fortune – for women as well as for men.

Volcano

In dream lore, volcanoes are seen to represent carnal desire – where strong emotions may be held in check, yet bubble away beneath the surface, to be released in the inevitable, violent eruption of pent-up fury. Thus, to dream of an exploding volcano symbolizes unbridled lust – but carries with it the implicit warning that care should be taken lest "desire" turn to dangerous obsession.

Vultures

Their very names are synonymous with ill-omen, and to dream that vultures circle above you portends vicious competitors who are waiting to move in and take their pick. Their function of cleaning up rotting carrion, however, could be taken as a sign that your subconscious wishes to expunge some of the dead areas of your life.

A dream in which you see young and old walking hand-in-hand should be interpreted as an encouraging vision, the psyche's "alpha and omega," the symbol of "first and last" – your life's span.

Walk

Dreaming that you are walking in a deliberate and intentional manner denotes a desire to progress toward your personal ambitions and goal – but at a speed of your own choosing. The dream's symbolism further indicates that rewards will be reaped through individual effort and determination, but patience will be needed as your destiny will unfold before you at a slow, but steady, pace.

War

At a subconscious level, to dream of war (especially civil war) can suggest inner conflict – a battle between the dictates of the spirit and the desires of the flesh. Its aggressive energy represents the masculine aspect of the psyche, and may symbolize an initiation into manhood for the dreamer. As a dream omen, it is a harbinger of misfortune and illness foretelling dangerous times ahead for the security of a personal, or business, partnership.

Water

Water is among the most common dream subjects, and it has come to represent many things. Its connection with the uterine fluid of the womb, and its role in evolution, make it a symbol of emergent life. In dreams (as in baptism) to be immersed in water is to be cleansed and spiritually reborn. Indeed, since the earliest dream oracles, water has been regarded as a fortuitous omen – a sign of myriad blessings. To dream of spilling it, however, foretells a quarrel.

Waterfall

To dream of fast-flowing water denotes a sparkling vibrancy. Combine this with the raw energy symbolized by a waterfall, and the dreamer is offered the prospect of a lively and effervescent time.

"*Man is but the dream of a shadow*".

PYTHIAN ODE 8

"And dreaming through the twilight
That doth not rise nor set,
Haply I may remember,
And haply may forget."

CHRISTINA ROSSETTI 1830–94

Water lily

In many ancient cultures the lotus, or water lily, was considered a sacred flower. It was seen to embody the four elemental forces – Earth, from which it grew; Water, from whence it came; Air, in which it bloomed; and Fire at the burning heart of its blossom. To dream of water lilies foretells that your aspirations and wishes will always remain just out of your reach.

The water lily symbolizes that which is beyond reach. Likewise, those who dream of rough waves may, by their obduracy, place themselves beyond the reach of other people's affections.

Waves

In the world of sleep, waves represent emotions – their ebb and flow, rage or calm. To dream of waves on the sea is an omen of short-lived friendships; while those on a lake indicate intolerance. To imagine battling against the waves of a rough sea in your sleep suggests you are strong-willed and obstinate – which can be either a drawback or an asset, depending upon circumstance.

Wealth

The morality of our sub-conscious does not always reflect the aspirations of our waking life. The prospect of amassing tremendous wealth might delight us when awake, but in our dreams our subconscious chooses to remind us of the old adage *"to die rich is to die disgraced."* So you should seek to use money for the greater good, not for the good of the great!

A famous dream of paradox – the more money the dreamer imagines they have, the greater will be its loss.

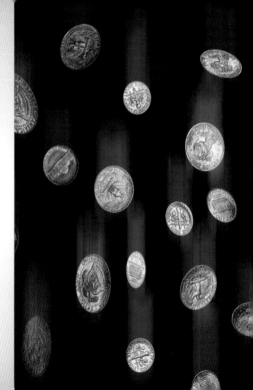

To dream of using **Weapons** weapons to harm another person is viewed as a metaphor for inner conflict. There may be elements of frustration or aggression that lie unaddressed – a clash between intellect and emotion, often related to the psyche's notion of sexuality. If you dream that the weapon is turned against yourself, be vigilant lest you inflict self-injury – the classic example of "shooting yourself in the foot."

Web

The web is rich in dream symbolism. To the Celts it was the web which held all life together, for the Egyptians and Ancient Greeks it represented the "web of being," and in Christian folklore the web symbolized the snare of the Devil.

In the iconography of dreams, a spider's web represents the binding ties of the home. These may be experienced by the dreamer as feelings of being trapped – tied to domestic routine yet bound by a feeling of anxiety to leave it.

Weight and Dieting

In dreams we sometimes deliberately exaggerate facets of our bodies that we think are in need of change. Thus, to dream of being overweight (or too thin) may be your mind's way of prompting you to consider the option of a healthier diet. Sometimes a dream about dieting may have little to do with physical weight. Rather it could be interpreted as a sign to "tighten your belt" due to money problems.

Well

The ability to draw the precious gift of water from the earth invests the well with potent dream symbolism. It is traditionally accorded the power to heal and grant wishes.

To see a well in your dream is indeed a fortunate omen, and to quench your thirst from its mysterious depths is taken as a sign that one day you will develop psychic gifts. To offer a token (a coin, a nut, or a stone) implies your acceptance of "fate," which in return, will bless you and cause fortune to smile on you.

Whale

The dream symbolism of this beguiling giant finds an echo in the legend of Jonah, who was swallowed by a whale and emerged from its belly spiritually reborn. In dream lore, the whale has feminine significance because of its spacious body cavities – in some quarters it is known as the "womb of Mother Nature." Thus, to dream of a whale can indicate a spiritual journey in which the dreamer is replenished from the store of the unconscious, to be born anew.

Wheat

A symbol of riches representing the fertility of the Earth, and, even more auspiciously, of the inner fertility of the enlightened mind. In the religious lore of the Ancient Greeks, ears of ripe corn were considered to be the offspring of the Sun and the Earth. They promise the dreamer the assured love of a joyous companion.

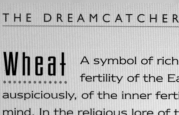

In dreams the wheel has deep symbolic importance. It represents the ever-turning,

Wheel

ever-changing circle of life, whose constant motion – though it may lead through all points of the compass – is destined to return it to its original position. Thus, it is indicative of life, death, decay, and rebirth. In dreams, the swifter the motion of its turning, the sooner will matters be returned to normal.

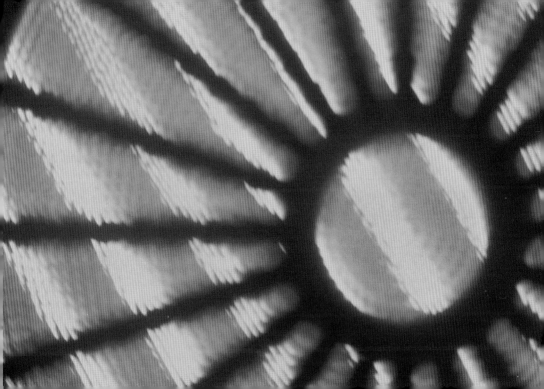

Wild Flowers

Wild flowers are among the purest expressions of joy known to the human spirit. They have no flavor of eternity; they bloom and fade to haunt us with their impermanence. As an omen in dreams, they represent the qualities of beauty and the vibrancy of nature. Even the short life of a bloom, and its inevitable dying, serves merely as a warning against over-confidence. To dream you pick and gather wild flowers signifies great joy, and to receive a posy foretells an open-spirited suitor. In short, wild flowers are among the most pleasurable of subjects about which we dream.

Try to place this dream in **Wind**
context – a light wind presages
an opportune moment to begin a new
venture, whereas strong gusts of wind
signal an unsettling period ahead. The
wind may also represent the freedom of
your inner spirit, and harnessing it – as in
the symbol of the windmill – should be
regarded as a most encouraging vision.

A dream vision similar to
the image of mountain
flowers (left) suggest
favorable omens – a breeze
(opportunity) gently stirs
the heads of wild flowers
(vitality and beauty).

Winter

To dream of this season indicates a period of rest and contemplation. You should consider your past triumphs and disasters, and learn to draw solace from the former and wisdom from the latter. Winter may also be seen as a period of inner-growth – a time to reach deep within yourself for endurance and fortitude.

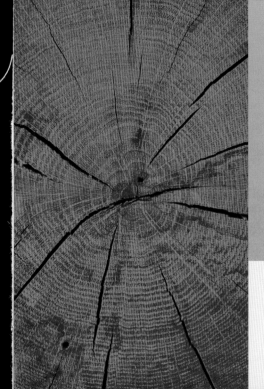

Wood
Wood as a dream symbol shows that through strength of character, and strength of arm, will come just reward. To see yourself chopping or cutting wood bodes well for a contented family life, albeit one achieved by hard toil. To dream that you burn wood indicates admirers – if the wood is green and will not light, the admirer is emotionally immature; if the fire smokes, they will be too old.

The measured passage of the years revealed graphically in the grain of timber, as tree rings, may appear as a device in our dreams to symbolize the passage of time.

Dreams concerning work are likely to reveal the influence of **Work** the problems currently facing you in real life. Your subconscious may deliberately exaggerate pressure at work to try to force a waking decision; or simply to act as a safety valve, releasing built-up tension and anxieties.

Wreath A wreath seen in a dream combines the powerful symbolism of the flower with that of the ring – a binding together of this world and the next (as evident in a funerary wreath). A garland of fresh flowers in a dream forebodes either interesting news, or fleeting pleasure; whereas a withered wreath signifies wounded love. Having a wreath placed on your head symbolizes hard-won success attained despite malice and jealousy.

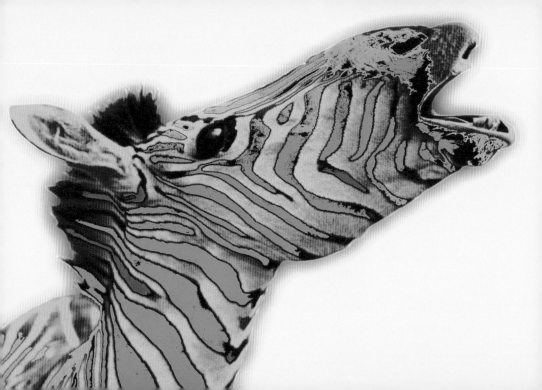

Zebra Beasts of contradiction and ill omen. You should be warned when dreaming about these creatures to keep your eyes wide open at all times, and to remain alert to the threat of danger and duplicity. Their presence can also denote interest in fleeting enterprises that will lead to nothing but financial loss and vexation.

The images of the 12 signs of the **Zodiac** zodiac were originally linked with the heavenly constellations. They were symbolized graphically in Arabic texts; and to study them in dreams means that you will gain recognition for your achievements, especially in the eyes of strangers. As with astrologers of old, you may gain insight into those things hidden from mortal eyes, and with this new knowledge succeed in your endeavors to your own astonishment, and the delight of others.

Index